IMMIGRANT
ENTREPRENEURSHIP
IN AMERICA

Insights from the Journey to Success

GORM TUXEN

FOREWORD BY JACK STACK,
BEST SELLING AUTHOR OF THE GREAT GAME OF BUSINESS

Immigrant Entrepreneurship In America:
Insights from the Journey to Success

Copyright © Gorm Tuxen (2026)

All rights reserved. No part of this publication may be reproduced, stored in a retrieval system, or transmitted, in any form or by any means, without the prior written permission of the publisher.

ISBN Paperback: 979-8-89576-176-2
ISBN Hardback: 979-8-89576-175-5

Published by:

Dedication

This book is dedicated to the founding fathers of our great nation. They had the wisdom to understand that building a nation offered people from all over the world an opportunity to come and contribute to the American Experiment through hard work and sacrifice, while building a better life for themselves and their families.

To our fellow citizens: thank you for welcoming us as part of this beautiful country. We are one more brick in the foundation forged by every immigrant and their descendants who labored, served, fought, and died for this country, building it brick by brick in just 250 years.

Thank God for the American Dream!

Table of Contents

Foreword 7

Introduction 9

Chapter 1 - My Story 13

Chapter 2 - Changing Paths 28

Chapter 3 - Reinventing Myself in a Changing America 33

Chapter 4 - American Immigrants 40

Chapter 5 - Immigration Policy 47

Chapter 6 - Learning Beyond the Classroom 54

Chapter 7 - Challenge and Response 63

Chapter 8 - Expectations and Outcomes 67

Chapter 9 - Building Beyond the Blueprint 71

Chapter 10 - Work Versus Play and Fulfillment 76

Chapter 11 - Virtualism vs. Realism 80

Chapter 12 - The Pillars of Growth 84

Chapter 13 - Paying It Forward 88

Chapter 14 - NEDAP Consulting and Technology 93

Chapter 15 - The Entrepreneurial Journey 102

Chapter 16 - The International Business Journey 120

Chapter 17 - Sales: The Journey from Value to Victory 126

Chapter 18 - Business Growth and Maturity 132

Chapter 19 - Emergency Management: Spin Control 141

Chapter 20 - Meaningful Rewards 145

Epilogue - A Tribute 149

Acknowledgements 153

Foreword

By Jack Stack
Author of *The Great Game of Business*
CEO, SRC Holdings

When I first heard about this book, I expected a case study filled with data and arguments about the importance of immigration to the future of the United States. I envisioned statistics on declining birth rates, an aging workforce, labor shortages in essential industries, and projections indicating that we may not have enough people working to sustain our economy by 2030. I thought I'd be reading about the gap that needs to be filled, whether by increasing productivity, embracing artificial intelligence, or welcoming more immigrants.

However, this book takes a unique and far more compelling approach. It doesn't dwell on charts or forecasts. Instead, it weaves a narrative about the immigrant as a real person. It's a story of the struggles, determination, and resilience of an individual who came to America, faced the obstacles, and still found a way to contribute and thrive. It's a poignant reminder that the American Dream is real, but it demands extraordinary perseverance, faith, and relentless hard work.

More than just a personal journey, this book is a practical playbook. It shows readers what it takes to pursue a dream and hold onto it, even after being knocked down time and again. It's a testament to how resilience, belief, and commitment to family and community can empower someone to get back up and start over—again and again—until success finally comes.

What moved me most in these pages is how clearly the author reveals the humanity of immigrants: the kindness, humility, and generosity of people who often live modestly, yet would gladly share their last meal with a stranger. These are the men and women who dedicate their lives to their families, who respect others simply for being human, and who quietly make positive contributions that strengthen our nation every day. This emphasis on immigrants' positive contributions will foster appreciation and respect among readers.

Gorm's story is both inspiring and instructive. It's not just about his personal triumphs, but also about the broader truth: immigration has always been one of America's greatest strengths. By sharing his journey so openly and authentically, the author has given us a gift, a reminder to respect, appreciate, and honor the neighbors who continue to help make America a land of opportunity. This is a beautiful book, and I am proud to recommend it.

Introduction

The first time I saw an iceberg, I wasn't thinking about how cold it was.

I was thinking about how far I'd come.

It was July 1975, and I peered out the airplane window south of Greenland, halfway to America. The jagged white giants below seemed to mirror my emotions: massive, awe-inspiring, and impossible to ignore. That moment had been a year in the making.

It all began in the quiet Danish town of Jyderup, with a population of 3,000, during my final year of high school. One summer afternoon in 1974, a single poster on the school bulletin board changed everything. It was an invitation from the International Cultural Exchange (ICX): *Spend your senior year in America as a foreign exchange student.* I didn't know it yet, but answering that call would shape the rest of my life.

That year had already tested my family. In February, we survived a near-catastrophic car accident. My dad lay in the hospital with his left leg nearly destroyed. From his bed, he tried to keep the family business afloat, dictating ideas to his partner. My mom was severely injured as well. At sixteen, I suddenly became the head of the household, with my grandmother's help, looking after my brother and sister while trying to maintain some semblance of normalcy.

I had been in the front seat next to my father during the accident and somehow walked away with only light injuries. But overnight, I had gone from a teenager to an adult. That experience didn't make me a victim; it made me a victor. I realized I had responsibilities to shoulder, and I found an extraordinary strength inside myself to meet them. That strength, that resilience, has stayed with me ever since, a reminder of the human spirit's ability to rise, even when everything seems broken.

So when I read that poster on the wall, my perspective had already shifted. I knew this was my chance. I began my application that very day. I didn't yet understand the full weight of what I was choosing, the culture shock, the language barriers, the challenges that would come, but I knew it was the right step. As I gazed down at those icebergs on the flight to America, I wondered what lay in store for me.

That was in 1974. I could never have imagined how that single decision would shape the course of my life. What followed was a journey beyond anything I had dreamed: a path filled with challenges, unexpected blessings, and opportunities that continue to unfold, even now.

I arrived in Memphis knowing almost nothing about the United States, stepping into the sweltering Tennessee heat to meet my host parents for the first time. My preparations had given me the basics, but nothing could prepare me for the lifelong adventure that awaited.

What I discovered was a life richer than I ever expected, a journey that included setbacks and triumphs, defeats and victories, each one shaping me into who I am today. Just like the icebergs I saw from that plane, our lives are shaped by what lies beneath the surface: the experiences, choices, and perspectives that define us.

That's what this book is about. Not just my story, but what it means to take risks, endure challenges, and find strength in unlikely places. It's about the resilience of immigrants, the grit of entrepreneurs, and the universal truth that, while obstacles are inevitable, our response shapes our destiny.

I'm writing this book with the hope that my perspective may spark your own reflections on what brings you happiness, fulfillment, and success. By sharing my experiences, I invite you to consider your own, realizing that perspective itself is the first part of every new chapter.

Join me on this road to success. Together, we'll reflect on challenges faced, obstacles overcome, and lessons learned along the way. Your journey, with all its victories and defeats, matters. And perhaps, like me staring down at those icebergs, you'll discover that the distance you've traveled is as awe-inspiring as the destination ahead.

CHAPTER 1

My Story

I still remember the smell of sawdust in my father's workshop. It clung to his hands, to his clothes, to the air itself. That shop was more than a place of work; it was a classroom. It was where I first learned the value of hard work, discipline, and the quiet pride that comes from building something with your own two hands.

I was born on a frigid New Year's Eve in 1957, just outside Copenhagen, the son of Viggo and Lily Tuxen. My earliest memories are faint, but my mother's photographs remind me of the warmth that filled our small home. My father, a carpenter by trade, had just started his first company with his mentor, proudly painting "Tuxen Master Carpenter" on the side of their first work van. My parents were young, ambitious, and determined to build a better life than the one they had inherited.

That resilience was not theoretical; it was forged in the face of hardship. My father's family had survived the Nazi occupation of Denmark. My mother grew up fatherless after her own dad, a resistance member, was shot gathering intelligence near the harbor in 1944. She was only seven years old. Her widowed mother raised her on a seamstress's wages and a small pension, instilling in her the quiet strength of survival without complaint.

From both sides of my family, I inherited a stubborn determination: to endure, to build, and to hope. Though I didn't yet understand it, resilience was already in my bloodline.

Roots of Resilience

My father came from a family of four boys and two girls. While two of his brothers stayed under their father's careful guidance in the family business, he was cut from a different cloth, restless, curious, and eager to see the world. That wanderlust carried him to sea as a sailor, until one brutal voyage off the British coast left him so seasick that he swore off sailing as a career.

Around the same time, fate intervened. At a family gathering, my grandmother, who was a friend of my mother's family, introduced him to the young woman who would change his course entirely. My father's adventures ended not in a shipwreck but in something more substantial: love. He married young, built a home, and committed himself to family and business.

Both sides of my family knew hardship. My paternal grandfather, a self-made merchant, expanded a modest family venture into a successful business while surviving Nazi occupation. My maternal grandmother, widowed in her thirties, relied on her pension and a modest income as a seamstress to raise her daughter. They were graduates of what I call the School of Hard Knocks. Their lives were defined by resilience, not by choice but by necessity.

Without complaint or bitterness, they built a secure future from the rubble of history. That quiet heroism shaped me more than I realized at the time. It also set the stage for my own journey, one that would require the same resilience in ways I could not yet imagine.

Golden Days and New Challenges

My maternal grandmother never remarried. By the time I came along, she spoiled me in the best ways through love, patience, and stories that carried the weight of our family's past. My step-grandfather, meanwhile, became my partner in mischief, always ready for small adventures my parents might not have approved of.

By 1961, my sister Ulla was born, and I stepped into the role of proud big brother. Four years later, my father took a job managing a summer home construction factory, part of Denmark's post-war building boom. That opportunity moved us to the small town of Jyderup, with a population of 3,000, a place that would define my formative years.

In 1967, my brother Lau arrived, completing our family of five. My parents, always striving for higher goals, enrolled me in a private school. They hoped it would give me a head start, but the school also housed troubled youths from Copenhagen, and the environment was more about survival than learning. For five long years, I endured bullying, which tested me in ways I hadn't expected.

One memory from that time still makes me smile: my English teacher, dodging airborne objects in class, muttering over and over, "Where der is a will, der is a way." I'm still not sure whether she was trying to teach us or convince herself she'd survive the lesson.

Looking back, those years taught me something invaluable: resilience isn't always about winning. Sometimes it's about enduring. Those lessons, though painful, planted seeds of strength I would lean on in the years to come.

Building Independence

Public school gave me room to breathe. After years of looking over my shoulder, I could finally turn my attention inward. Still, I struggled to concentrate in class, my mind a whirlwind of adventures while the teacher droned on about math equations or grammar. None of it seemed to connect to anything real or important for my future. But Lego did. I built elaborate worlds, each brick a step beyond Jyderup, each creation a doorway to something bigger. In those imagined futures, I found both control and possibility.

My father, never one to sit still for long, soon co-founded another company with a colleague and former boss. To fund it, my parents sold our Audi, mortgaged the house, and bought a well-worn sedan. We became intimately familiar with porridge, liver, rice pudding, and scratchy toilet paper. My mother became the company's accountant, her first job outside the home, while my younger brother often played in the factory during school hours.

For me, these years brought another challenge. I began to suffer from chronic stomach issues, and eventually, I was diagnosed with ulcerative colitis, a condition with no cure at the time. It complicated every part of my life. Some days, it felt impossible to keep up. But even then, I worked because working felt like living.

My first job was delivering vegetables for a greengrocer, pedaling a massive bike loaded with produce through the streets of town. Later, I joined my father in the factory, where we turned raw lumber into siding and ceiling panels. Craftsmanship became my quiet teacher, instilling in me a pride that came not from what I was paid, but from what I created.

Those years were lean, but they taught me something no classroom ever could: independence is built one responsibility at a time. Each job, each sacrifice, each setback carried its own lesson, adding another layer to the resilience I would one day need.

My First Taste of Enterprise

By high school, I was ready to test my independence in new ways. One afternoon, as I sped through town on my bicycle, a man in a car followed me and finally pulled over. "I've never seen anyone ride a bike that fast," he said. Then he offered me a job delivering newspapers.

It turned out to be more than a delivery job. I also had to sell subscriptions and collect payments. My mother, ever resourceful, stepped in to handle the accounting, and together we turned it into a profitable little enterprise. That experience opened my eyes: work could be more than a wage. It could be a business.

Around the same time, I formed my first real friendship. My new friend Ebbe was a gifted athlete, and in exchange for my help with schoolwork, he helped me develop an interest in physical training. We idolized Arnold Schwarzenegger, working out daily with a knock-off Bullworker in basements and back rooms. That friendship transformed me. I grew stronger in body and mind, and for the first time, I began to believe in my own potential.

By my senior year, my life had undergone significant changes. The shy, withdrawn boy had given way to a confident young man who finally understood the relevance of school. I poured myself into my studies, driven not by obligation but by a growing sense of purpose. The fears that once held me back were fading, replaced by ambition.

I set my sights on a single goal: becoming a fighter pilot in the Danish Air Force. Every subject I studied, every assignment I completed, was measured against that dream. For the first time, my efforts were not about proving others wrong; they were about preparing myself for the future I could now see so clearly.

Looking back, those teenage years were a turning point. Delivering papers taught me the basics of business. Friendship and fitness taught me discipline. And aiming for the sky as a pilot gave me the confidence to pursue something greater. Even then, the threads of resilience, entrepreneurship, and ambition were beginning to weave together.

A Turning Point

In February 1974, everything changed.

We were driving when, in an instant, a car traveling the wrong way slammed into us head-on. The sound of metal crushing and glass shattering was deafening. Then came silence, the kind of silence that stretches, heavy and surreal, as if the world itself has stopped.

My father was severely injured, and so was my mother. I had been in the front seat next to my father, and though I walked away with only minor injuries, I was not the same person. At that moment, my childhood ended. I saw how fragile life really is.

The accident forced me to grow up quickly. Responsibilities at home became heavier, and the carefree lens of youth was replaced with the sober realization that time is not guaranteed. I carried those lessons with me into everything that came after, into school, into work, and eventually into my leap across the Atlantic.

My mother returned home after head surgery about two weeks later, still wrapped in bandages and struggling through recovery. She bravely tried to take charge of the family, but she needed time to heal and spend time at the hospital with my father, who remained bedridden for almost a year. My maternal grandmother stepped in, and together we did our best to keep the household running.

For me, this meant helping my younger brother and sister with chores, supporting my mother and grandmother however I could, and managing my own chores. The responsibility didn't feel like a burden—it felt like purpose. In some way, I took pride in being part of piecing our family back together. The prospect of what we could have lost made me value them even more, and it built a strength inside me that I hadn't known was there.

Those months taught me how to shoulder responsibility and find meaning in service. They showed me that adversity could harden you, but it could also forge resilience. That strength became part of me, a quiet preparation for the bigger leap that lay ahead.

By the time my father regained stability and our family life was back under control, I knew it was time to pursue the adventure that had been calling me.

In August 1975, I boarded a plane bound for the United States. The contrast could not have been sharper. After the darkness of that accident, stepping off the plane into the sweltering Memphis heat felt like stepping into another world, one filled with optimism, openness, and freedom.

Being foreign was no longer a burden. In America, it became an asset. Strangers leaned in, curious about my accent, my background, and my story. I felt a sense of belonging I hadn't expected, and it set the stage for friendships that remain part of my chosen family to this day.

The accident took something from me, but it also gave me something else: perspective. It taught me that life can change in an instant. And it reminded me that if I was going to chase dreams, I had to do it fully and without hesitation.

Crossing the Atlantic

Halfway across the ocean, I peered out the window and saw icebergs drifting south of Greenland. Jagged and silent, they mirrored the mix of fear and wonder inside me.

I wasn't just crossing an ocean. I was crossing into a new life.

As I stepped off the plane in Memphis, a wave of thick, scorching heat wrapped around me, heavy and stifling, nothing like the crisp, cool air of Denmark. My host parents were waiting at the gate, smiling and curious, ready to welcome me into their lives. I had studied the language and prepared for cultural differences, but nothing could prepare me for the feeling of standing there. I was foreign yet free, uncertain yet alive with possibility.

For the first time, being different felt like an advantage. My accent drew people in. My story opened doors. In America, curiosity replaced suspicion, openness replaced judgment, and optimism, palpable in every conversation, made me feel, in some strange way, at home.

Within a few weeks, I was enrolled at Bishop Byrne High School in Whitehaven, a sprawling suburb of Memphis. It was a Catholic school, and though I was Lutheran by default, as most Danes were, I felt immediately accepted. My electives reflected everything I wanted to learn differently in America: Civics, English, American History, and Physical Education. Each subject opened a window into a culture I was eager to understand.

The first day of school began with a tour led by two cheerleaders, a welcome that boosted my confidence more than they realized.

Everything was new: the lockers, the cinder block walls painted in school colors, the fashion of Earth Shoes and flared pants. It was like drinking from a fire hose, each detail another reminder that I was no longer in Denmark. Even learning to tie a double knot in my wide tie became part of adapting to this new world.

Slowly, I found my place. Lunch in the Commons became the center of my social life, and I was welcomed into conversations, classrooms, and friendships. I resonated most with those who were curious, ambitious, and bright, classmates who became my stewards in this foreign land. Over time, two of them, Gene and Dan, grew into lifelong friends. Their families embraced me as their own, and by the end of the year, I spent more time in their homes than with my host parents. They became my American family, a safety net that would support me long after my exchange year ended.

The year wasn't without its humorous moments. At graduation in 1976, my gown, mismeasured in the conversion from metric to U.S. sizes, came up far too short. I walked across the stage looking like I was wearing a miniskirt, but I wore it proudly.

By the end of that year, I had no desire to return to Denmark. I had discovered something profound: relevance. In a place thousands of miles from home, I had found myself more alive, more connected, and more at home than I had ever felt before. That exchange year didn't just shape my English; it shaped my identity and set the stage for my return as an adult.

Coming "Home"

Coming back to Denmark, I was filled with mixed emotions. While I enjoyed being with my family, my soul lingered behind in America. I was severely homesick for my new adoptive country. My dreams had materialized into lifelong friendships and an understanding of America that far exceeded my wildest expectations.

My two best friends from high school would soon follow me to Denmark to have their own limited exchange experience with our family. Sharing regular audio recordings became a ritual for years to come.

I had left for America with a dream of being proficient enough in English to join the Danish Air Force; unfortunately, at the time, recruitment was partially based on the national draft. As it turns out, my draft session had passed while I was in the United States. Fortunately, I avoided arrest, but I lost my chance to be an Air Force Pilot.

Preparing for the Leap

I entered college disillusioned, still stung by the loss of the Air Force opportunity. Denmark, like much of the world, was undergoing rapid social change. The Cold War was at its height, and Soviet propaganda, touting the supposed benefits of socialism and communism, was ubiquitous. Danish colleges became fertile ground for these ideas, and debates raged daily.

Returning from the United States, I had witnessed the stark contrast between our values and those of the Americans. That clarity fueled a conviction: I would immigrate to America. From that moment on, every choice became a building block toward that goal.

After two years in public college, debating my way through every waking hour without making a dent, I realized my path needed to change. I was meant to be a businessman. It had been right in front of me all along, woven into my upbringing in the family trade. A liberal arts degree wasn't going to take me there, so I retooled by spending another year at business school, studying subjects that would prepare me for the future I envisioned.

Those years of disillusionment and discovery forced me to reassess what I truly wanted from life. The foundation of resilience, family sacrifice, and a restless drive for something more had carried me this far, but I was about to enter a new phase.

In the next chapter, "Changing Paths," I'll share how those early lessons prepared me to navigate unexpected detours and redefine success on my own terms. My story may be unique, but the principles are universal. This book isn't only about where I've been, it's about the insights and practices that can help you face your own crossroads with clarity, resilience, and purpose.

In the years that followed, I returned to Denmark to complete my education, get married, and start building a future. Yet even then, I sensed that my path would not remain there forever. Those early lessons were preparing me for a larger leap, one that would carry me back across the Atlantic for good. Just as those icebergs once reminded me, what shapes us most lies beneath the surface, unseen but powerful enough to change the course of a life.

From Thesis to Opportunity

As I was finishing my second degree, I searched everywhere for a company that might send me to the United States. After weighing several options, I chose a small, privately owned hardwood import firm in Copenhagen. They didn't send me to America; I was dispatched to Bavaria in southern Germany to quality-sort beech logs for the British furniture industry. I perfected my German and learned a great deal, but my ultimate goal still felt out of reach.

Not long after, another door opened. A new private school for adult education, established by local businessmen, launched an ambitious program: a master's degree in International Marketing and Export Management at the Danish School of International Marketing and Management in Herning (Den Danske Exportskole 1979–2001). The program was a grueling eighteen months: intense language study, a trial thesis, and a final thesis defended in an oral presentation. Failure at any step meant starting over from scratch.

I applied and was accepted for the school year starting in August 1980, the second class launched by the new school.

We, the students, were even responsible for our own recruitment through a student-led organization. Our task was to secure company sponsors for market studies abroad. At the time, furniture was Denmark's leading export, so I arranged a meeting with the president of the Danish Furniture Association. We successfully placed all 30 students, with most finding employment in the furniture industry.

My friend Jens and I came up with the idea of selling Christmas trees in the center of town. It was more than just a fundraiser; it was our crash course in sales, logistics, and stamina. We hustled through freezing evenings, with the biting wind often stealing our breath, as we convinced busy families to buy from a group of scrappy students. By the end of the season, the money we raised not only covered outreach expenses but also proved that, with creativity and grit, we could open doors beyond our reach. The success of our bootstrapped efforts gave me the confidence to aim higher, and I was hooked on the entrepreneurial journey.

I kept my eye on the U.S. market and pursued Domino Furniture, Denmark's largest manufacturer. It was a long shot; no one had ever landed a sponsor that far away, but persistence paid off. After three meetings with their U.S. Sales Director and their Export Director, they agreed: my thesis would explore the feasibility of establishing a subsidiary in America. Suddenly, the stakes were real.

That summer of 1981, I immersed myself in research, spending hours at the U.S. Embassy Library and the Danish Trade Ministry, photocopying mountains of reports. On September 1, I left Copenhagen for Minneapolis and began driving through seven Midwestern states. Using nothing more than the Yellow Pages, I cold-called furniture stores not yet selling Scandinavian products. Over the course of a month, I compiled fifty surveys that formed the foundation of my thesis.

Back in Denmark, I threw myself into the project with everything I had. From early October 1981 until final exams in late November, I lived on little more than coffee and adrenaline, researching, analyzing, typing, and retyping late into the night. By the time I walked into my oral defense, six years of preparation came down to one presentation. When the results were announced, I learned I had graduated at the top of my class, an outcome I could only attribute to divine providence.

The announcement was made publicly in the school hallway. Almost immediately, my sponsors called. They wanted me to lead the new U.S. subsidiary, but under one condition: no interviews with the press. The next graduate in line received the media spotlight. I chose opportunity over fame.

1981 became a banner year. I had earned my degree, secured my dream assignment in the United States, and, along the way, met Anette, whose blonde hair and Kansas bow tie had made an unforgettable first impression.

Every ending is the beginning of a new path—
if you're willing to take the step.

A Partner in the Journey

During my studies, I also pursued the attention of a young woman named Anette, seven years my junior. By God's grace, she eventually agreed to join me in America. After completing her bachelor's degree, she moved into a small apartment with me in Racine, Wisconsin. It wasn't glamorous; we lived next door to a former mafia hitman in a rough part of town, but it was ours. My boss, knowing she was coming, generously allowed me to furnish the apartment with furniture from our new warehouse. Still, he ensured that I only earned money when I was out on the road selling.

Anette and I explored the Midwest together as I crisscrossed the region, calling on every furniture store I could find and placing product orders one by one.

In late 1983, after spending more than a year traveling back and forth, we returned to Denmark for Christmas. By then, it was clear we were meant for each other. Anette had grown more comfortable with life in America and the possibility of making it her home. At the same time, my company began working with the American embassy in Copenhagen to secure a change in her immigration status as a new employee at Domino Furniture. Everything seemed promising.

I went back to work in Racine in January 1984, expecting her to follow soon after. But late that month, while on a sales trip in Champaign–Urbana, I received news that upended our plans. The embassy had not only denied the change in status but also issued a three-month travel ban, preventing her from entering the United States.

Distraught, I cancelled my appointments and drove through a snowstorm back to Racine. By the time I arrived, it was late afternoon in Wisconsin and early morning in Denmark. I called Anette. She was just nineteen. What began as a conversation about visas quickly turned into a deeper discussion of our commitment and whether she could truly envision a life with me in America.

The answer was yes. Over the course of a three-hour phone call, I proposed marriage, laying out the challenges we would face, the sacrifices required, and the determination it would take to make it work. Ultimately, the decision was made. To soften the blow for her family, I made sure roses were delivered to her in Denmark the next morning. I knew my future mother-in-law would not be pleased with me.

In May 1984, we were married in Denmark. From that day forward, Anette became not only my wife but also my fellow immigrant and partner in this journey. Through sacrifice, resilience, and no small amount of courage, she embraced America as her own. Over time, she built her own success here, proving herself an entrepreneur in her own right.

With our commitment to each other secured, I turned back to the work still before me. Building a life together in America would require more than determination: it demanded opportunity.

CHAPTER 2

Changing Paths

Leaving home, embracing risk, and navigating culture shock: this chapter explores my journey to America and the transformational process of becoming an American.

Sometimes the only way forward is to leave everything familiar behind.

In 1982, I stepped onto American soil carrying equal measures of hope and illness. Ulcerative colitis had shadowed me for years, but I was determined to build a new life. Leaving Denmark wasn't just a relocation; it was a deliberate act of rewriting my future in a country that rewarded risk and resilience.

In February 1982, I stepped off a transatlantic flight at Chicago O'Hare with a suitcase full of ambition and a body wrecked by illness. The ulcerative colitis I had tried so hard to ignore had chosen this moment, perhaps out of poetic irony, to make its presence known. I was sick most of the way over, both from the disease and the overwhelming reality of what I was about to attempt. Leaving Denmark unraveled the familiar and marked the beginning of a slow, deliberate remaking of identity. I was determined to push through, wounded but resolute.

An older Danish-American gentleman was waiting at the gate. He had helped lay the foundation for the U.S. offices and warehouse of the Danish freight forwarding company with whom we were going to co-locate inventory and offices, paving the way for other Danish companies to establish a presence in the American Midwest. As we drove toward Racine, Wisconsin, I tried to push through the fog of fatigue and illness, peppering him with questions about what lay ahead. It was part curiosity, part survival instinct.

We arrived at the Holiday Inn, where I collapsed into bed and didn't stir again until Monday morning, my first official day on the job. I was weak and groggy, but I had come too far to let anything derail me now. The truth is, I had hidden my condition from my employers. Had they known the extent of it, I doubt I would have been given the opportunity in the first place. But I believed then, and still do, that sometimes it's better to step into the arena wounded than to wait for perfect conditions that may never come.

That afternoon, the same gentleman invited me to a Rotary Club meeting. I didn't know it yet, but this gathering would become the unlikely hinge upon which everything turned. Racine was one of the oldest Danish settlements in the United States, and the meeting room buzzed with a legacy of local influence. I was introduced as the "new arrival from Denmark," and suddenly I was surrounded by faces that looked like mine yet spoke with an unmistakably American rhythm. I was overwhelmed, disoriented, and still ill.

As fate would have it, one of the Rotarians in attendance was a gastroenterologist. He took me in and stabilized my condition, allowing me to return to work the next day. This twist of grace, pure serendipity wrapped in human kindness, was the first of many such moments that would define my American journey. It's a powerful reminder of the impact of community and the connections that can change our lives, reinforcing my belief in the strength of collective support.

My new office was a shared, open-floor space in the freight company's headquarters, a makeshift command post from which I was expected not to sit but to roam. I had been tasked with building a parallel dealer network for Danish furniture, an assignment equal parts exhilarating and impossible. My boss's instructions had been clear: "Go to America, make some money in the first year, and come home and ask for a raise, or just come home." That was the deal.

Buying a car was my first rite of passage. In Denmark, owning a car was a luxury. In America, it was a necessity. I negotiated a mileage reimbursement and bought my first vehicle, putting 77,000 miles on it in the first year. The road became both my workspace and my classroom. It was a baptism by highway.

Our greatest early triumph came in Chicago, where we onboarded Wicks Furniture, then one of the largest chains in the country. What began as a modest Scandinavian gallery in a grandfathered showroom soon expanded across their national footprint. Each new gallery was a quiet act of validation, a reminder that hard work still meant something in this country.

But as is often the case, success and disruption walk hand in hand.

In 1984, my closest colleague and the company's U.S. Sales Manager left to join a competitor. His replacement was a schoolteacher with no experience. It stung, not just because I had been overlooked, but because

I soon learned that the new hire and my former colleague were a couple, and my direct boss was planning to leave and join them. The ground beneath me was shifting again.

I had, thankfully, secured permanent residency for my wife and myself through my father's birthright citizenship. So I stayed the course. I wasn't done yet, not by a long shot.

In 1986, I took a leap of faith. I left the comfort of employment and invested everything I had, every dollar of saved bonuses, in opening a Scandinavian furniture store in Nashville. I became the majority partner, along with my two former bosses, in this venture. My wife, newly appointed Vice President of Sales, stood beside me. We tightened our belts and launched a startup the old-fashioned way, on grit, goodwill, and more risk than sense. However, we were determined to succeed, regardless of the challenges that lay ahead.

It was a humbling education in failure. Our first location floundered. Advertising costs swallowed our profits, and foot traffic never materialized. We learned quickly that assumptions don't pay the rent. In 1987, we found salvation in the form of two eager young real estate investors. They gave us prime space on West End Avenue, and suddenly we were where we belonged, downtown, visible, and finally positioned to serve our ideal customers.

We had learned the hard truth of retail: location, location, location.

We pivoted toward a more upscale product line, aiming squarely at Nashville's young professionals until the economy took a turn. In the early 1990s, a new financial crisis gripped the country. Exchange rates flipped. Our customers lost their jobs. Our import model began to collapse under its weight. We had finally secured a $125,000 line of credit, but cash flow dried up. Meanwhile, my health deteriorated. The prednisone doses required to keep me upright were unsustainable.

In mid-1990, I underwent experimental surgery at the Lahey Clinic in Boston, an invasive, life-altering procedure that effectively rebuilt my digestive system. While still on a morphine drip, I renegotiated our bank credit line from my hospital bed. I told almost no one, not even my business partners.

I didn't want sympathy.

I wanted a path forward.

But in November 1990, the dam finally broke. Sales had stalled, debts had mounted, and our landlord found a new tenant. While still recovering, I met with the bank and offered them a deal: we'd liquidate the inventory and forfeit our pay until the debt was settled. Remarkably, they agreed. I was thrown out of my own office, but I walked away with my dignity intact.

We spent the next year cleaning up the wreckage. We were broke, but not bankrupt. We kept our home. We kept our names. And we kept moving.

I thought of my grandfather then, how he had left America during the Great Depression with empty pockets but a head held high. Like him, I had lost a great deal, but I refused to wear defeat.

I didn't come to America to quit.

I came to build.

CHAPTER 3

Reinventing Myself in a Changing America

In a twist of providence, a friend introduced me to a Taiwanese businessman in Nashville with deep ties to global trade. I wasn't given a job, but a chance, a stipend, and a seat at the table. I scoured telexes for trade leads, pitching everything from Levi's jeans in Russia to wooden pallets for German railways.

It was a grind.

However, in the fall of 1991, I saw a segment on CNN about a new in-car parking meter.

I was intrigued.

I tracked down the manufacturer, Duncan Industries in Harrison, Arkansas, and reached out to discuss potential business opportunities. With nothing but borrowed frequent flyer miles, I flew to Denmark and secured a meeting with the Copenhagen Department of Transportation. I didn't make a sale, but I did make an impression. Duncan was intrigued, and soon I was helping them explore an acquisition opportunity in Norway. In January 1992, I found myself negotiating with Norwegians in a snow-covered town called Hell.

My first invoice was paid just as my bank balance hit zero. For a moment, survival and opportunity collided, and I realized how thin the line could be between failure and a breakthrough.

Soon after, Duncan invited me to stay on as a consultant. My role was to develop new business models, explore emerging technologies, and reimagine what a parking meter could be in an increasingly digital world. It was my introduction to the global innovation economy, and it opened a door I hadn't even known existed.

It was there, in the midst of rethinking the future of parking, that I stumbled into the data revolution before it had a name.

I worked closely with regional salespeople, many of whom had just transitioned from independent distributors after Dover acquired the company. The air was heavy with apathy. Most saw the new electronic meter as a gimmick, a fancy piece of hardware with no real demand. I, too, was puzzled—that is, until the dime finally dropped, quite literally.

In listening to the old-timers swap war stories, a pattern emerged. The parking meter industry had long been riddled with opportunities for theft, both from the public and internally. City employees, some of whom were responsible for collecting and counting coins, had easy access and almost no oversight. Revenue from meters typically went into general municipal funds, bypassing scrutiny. That was the elephant in the room no one wanted to name.

Ironically, the very feature that made the new meter so innovative, its ability to track coins from the deposit to the counting room, was also its greatest liability for adoption.

Transparency was threatening.

This wasn't just about technology; it was about politics, habits, and fear.

Further complicating the matter was that meter operations, enforcement, and maintenance were typically handled by separate municipal departments, with little to no data integration. Vandalism was rampant, a modern-day phenomenon akin to *Cool Hand Luke.* And many mistakenly believed that a broken meter meant free parking, leading to deliberate damage.

By 1993, it became crystal clear: the value of the new meter wasn't in the hardware. It was in the potential for integrated data management. We weren't selling metal and circuit boards; we were selling accountability, insight, and the promise of reform. Back then, I used to call this "Risk Mitigation."

That realization shifted our entire strategy. Duncan expanded my role as a consultant and tasked me with identifying a software partner that could bring this vision to life. After months of research, we found a small, entrepreneurial company in Kalamazoo, Michigan. They had developed a citation management system for Western Michigan University and were eager to grow.

From this collaboration, Duncan Management Solutions was born. I negotiated the formation of this new division. I became its Vice President of Marketing and Sales, despite having no formal background in software or systems integration. This became my university.

We set out to transform parking management by building fully integrated platforms that tied meters, citations, maintenance, and revenue systems together. But adoption was slow. Our legacy Salesforce, still focused on hardware, lacked the appetite to promote what felt like a conceptual leap. Their loyalty was to volume, not vision.

In January 1996, I was named Director of Business Development and Engineering and relocated to our central production facility and HQ in Harrison, Arkansas.

When Duncan's president asked what we needed to break through, I proposed a targeted strategy: focus on the nation's largest cities: New York, Washington, DC, Los Angeles, and San Francisco. These were the municipalities that stood to gain the most from integration.

Fueled by purpose and supported by a president who believed in clearing bureaucratic hurdles, I began forging relationships in key cities. We moved purchasing decisions away from siloed departments and into centralized revenue offices, where our story made fiscal sense. Our integrity and persistence paid off.

By 2000, we had replaced hundreds of thousands of mechanical meters with smart devices across major cities. Entire fleets were modernized in DC, L.A., and New York. Revenue tripled. We weren't just a meter company anymore. We were redefining urban infrastructure.

But success attracts scrutiny. As contracts grew into the tens of millions, politics entered the picture. I found myself teeing off at mayoral golf tournaments, keeping our name visible in increasingly politicized procurement environments, always within the bounds of law, but not without a taste of disillusionment. I had come to America with ideals. I was learning how the sausage really got made.

By early 2001, the pressure mounted. My boss, a compassionate and principled man who had once left Dover Corporation to start a regional airline, was dismissed. He had bet on people like me. I owed much of my rise to his belief in my abilities.

Soon after, I was offered three new positions, each one a step backward in title or pay. On September 10, 2001, I declined them all and walked out, unsure of what would come next.

The very next morning, the world changed.

I watched in disbelief as the World Trade Center towers fell, the television screen flickering with images that felt impossible, unreal. Shock gave way to a heaviness I can still feel to this day, a weight of sorrow, fear, and uncertainty that left me standing still, powerless in my own living room.

And yet, in the middle of that tragedy, something unexpected happened. I felt at peace.

Not because I had answers—I didn't. Not because I had security—I had none. But because, in that moment, stripped of titles, paychecks, and plans, I realized none of it mattered compared to what I still had: my family, my faith, and the chance to rebuild with integrity.

The world had changed overnight.

I was unemployed, yes. But I was also strangely calm, as if the chaos had carved out a quiet space for clarity.

Amidst the tragedy, I discovered a stillness within myself, a reminder that peace doesn't come from circumstances. It comes from knowing who you are when everything else is taken away.

A corporate chapter had closed.

It was time to build again.

Within months, I launched Tuxen & Associates. My new home office overlooked a lake in Ridgedale, Missouri. The internet was finally coming into its own, and I poured myself into research. The events of 9/11 had made one thing clear: security and information integration would drive the next wave of innovation.

In 1997, my wife and I also welcomed our long-awaited daughter, a miracle and a reminder of what truly mattered. Her arrival rebalanced our world. My wife also stepped back into entrepreneurship, opening a boutique fashion store while continuing to support our home life with extraordinary commitment.

During the winter of 2001, I came across an article about virtual parking payments via mobile phone, a system thriving in Europe thanks to open telecom protocols. The article discussed NEDAP's involvement in this emerging technology area. NEDAP was a publicly listed Dutch electronics and software application company, established in 1929, with over 700 employees at the time.

The article, written by Evelien, marketing manager of the Identification Systems department, sparked something in me. I contacted her, booked flights on points, and drove to Groenlo, Netherlands, to meet the team.

This was to become the beginning of a truly transformational business relationship for both our companies, one that continues to grow to this day, a chapter on its own that I will talk more about later.

Tuxen & Associates became more than a company; it became a family. Today, two of my longest-serving employees have been promoted to Associate Partner. Together, we have become a trusted name across the Americas.

At the heart of it all was a belief I had carried from the beginning: success isn't about what you take. It's about what you build and who you build it for. It's about helping others grow.

Today, I am a mentor, a grandfather, and still an entrepreneur. I continue to invest, advise, and work alongside the next generation of builders. And I do it all with the same fire that brought me here: a desire to leave something better behind.

Because if there's one thing I've learned on this journey, it's that real opportunity isn't found. It's created brick by brick, deal by deal, relationship by relationship, by those willing to risk it all, fail fast, and start again.

I had left Denmark sick, uncertain, and unknown. I became an American entrepreneur the old way, by betting on myself, losing almost everything, and starting again. This chapter of my life taught me what resilience means, and that the American Dream is not a destination, but a fight to keep becoming.

My journey wasn't the first in my family. Long before me, another Tuxen crossed the Atlantic with little more than determination and the hope of a better future. His story, along with the stories of countless others, illustrates what it truly means to be an American immigrant. In Racine, I learned that belonging isn't something that's given; it's built, one connection at a time. With each step, I was becoming not just an immigrant in America, but an American in the making.

CHAPTER 4

American Immigrants

**The immigrant story is not about perfection.
It's about possibility.**

In 1926, my grandfather stepped off a ship onto American soil, carrying little more than determination and the hope of a better future. He was proud to be an immigrant, proud to contribute, and proud to claim his place in the fabric of a new country.

Like mine decades later, his journey was defined by hardship and resilience. More importantly, it embodied the immigrant mindset that has fueled America for generations: the belief that no matter where you start, you can build something lasting if you're willing to work and make sacrifices. Every immigrant carries a version of this story. **Some arrive by ship, some by plane, and others by the long road across borders, but all arrive with hope, uncertainty, and the desire to build.**

Give me your tired, your poor,
Your huddled masses yearning to breathe free.

This iconic line from Emma Lazarus's poem resonates deeply with me. It captures the American promise, not of handouts, but of opportunity. It's as relevant today as when it was first etched into the spirit of Ellis Island. **But promises are never passive. They invite action. The door may open—but only if you're willing to walk through it with full commitment.**

Opportunity comes with expectation.

Immigration is a privilege, not a right. When you seek citizenship, you're asking to be adopted into a new family, a nation that owes you nothing beyond a fair chance. It's only natural that this country expects your full commitment in return: to its laws, values, and community.

Throughout history, immigrants have been viewed as either burdens or blessings, depending on prevailing labor demand. At its core, the American dream doesn't guarantee success. It ensures the freedom to pursue it. And that's where the real power lies: in taking ownership of your future.

Despite the challenges and the blurred lens of politics, it's important to remember that this country was built by resilient immigrants who toiled and sacrificed for the betterment of their families and the country that had graciously welcomed them. Their resilience is a beacon of hope, inspiring us to face our challenges with courage and determination.

What has traditionally been asked of immigrants is simple: work hard and integrate. Learn the language, respect the laws, and become part of the cultural fabric. Do so not as an outsider demanding change, but as a willing contributor embracing it. Of course, not every immigrant wants that. Some arrive seeking only economic gain, without a desire to engage with the community. But the immigrants who flourish, the ones who are welcomed, trusted, and respected, are those who adopt a mindset of service over self.

Attitudes toward immigration often reflect the needs of the moment. During periods of economic growth, immigrants are frequently viewed as assets. In times of uncertainty, they become scapegoats. However, regardless of public opinion, the path to acceptance remains unchanged: **listen, learn, and lead by example.**

That principle applies to all of us, not just immigrants. The more we invest in understanding others, in earning our place rather than demanding it, the more fully we are accepted. Contribution builds credibility. Empathy fosters trust and a deeper understanding of the immigrant experience.

When we're consumed by survival, it's hard to think about belonging or higher aspirations. Maslow's hierarchy of needs teaches us that before we can focus on connection, self-esteem, or self-actualization, we must first secure our basic needs, such as food and safety. For many immigrants, the journey starts with meeting these fundamental needs in a new country. However, as they find stability, a transformation occurs as they begin contributing to their communities, creating opportunities, and helping to shape a better future. We stop reacting and start building.

Entrepreneurship plays a crucial role in this process. It's about embracing risk, finding self-confidence, and pursuing bold goals despite challenges. While immediate needs can feel all-consuming, building something greater requires a shift in focus from reacting to circumstances to taking action that creates lasting impact.

The American Dream is what makes bold risk-taking possible and sets this nation apart: the belief that, with effort, discipline, and courage, anyone can rise. Unlike many countries where immigration is seen as a threat to national identity, in America, at its best, it's an invitation to contribute to something greater. This belief emphasizes progress and self-reliance, encouraging immigrants to define themselves by their successes rather than the hardships or history they left behind. Overcoming challenges and relying on one's determination builds the strength and confidence needed to keep striving for improvement.

At the heart of the American Dream is the idea of personal agency: that we are not victims of circumstance, but victors through effort. Immigrants who embrace this mindset define themselves by progress, not by what they escaped, but by what they build.

Yes, many arrive with heavy burdens: war, poverty, persecution. But those who succeed here don't let their past define their future. They take responsibility. They act. And in doing so, they build strength, not just for themselves, but for the country they now call home.

Self-reliance becomes the cornerstone of contribution. That's why embracing a victim mentality, believing the world owes you something, can be so damaging. It doesn't just weaken motivation; it breeds resentment, both within individuals and among others. America thrives on mutual contribution, not passive consumption.

The goal isn't to erase who you were before you arrived. It's to channel that history into a new identity rooted in responsibility, resilience, and community.

Similar generalizations and sociological typecasting lead only to the formation of theoretical sandboxes, a metaphor for societal categorization based on characteristics beyond one's control. These "sandboxes" are very convenient for controlling the general populace, as they limit individual potential and perpetuate societal norms, creating barriers for immigrants and others to fully participate in and contribute to society.

America's status as an immigrant nation, by virtue of the foresight of our founding fathers and the Constitution that they so ably crafted, represents in my mind the highest level of aspiration to define rules to govern a truly free nation founded in individual freedoms, responsibilities, and laws. It is built on the core belief that individuals matter and can be trusted to form meaningful collaboration for the benefit of all.

In the international context, it is worth noting that America is the most prominent country to have fought and won the right to national independence at a time when royalty or emperors ruled large parts of the world.

This is where the American Dream was born, a country where you are allowed to dream and pursue your aspirations without being perceived as a pariah by others. The American Dream, a concept that embodies the belief that anyone, regardless of their background, can achieve their version of success in a society where upward mobility is possible, is a key part of the immigrant experience. However, you are also expected to apply self-governance, restraint, and compassion toward your fellow human beings. The American Dream serves as a powerful motivator, inspiring us to strive for success and upward mobility.

My grandfather was an American immigrant. In January 1926, he left his native Denmark and his fiancée behind to chase a dream across the Atlantic, his destination being Askov, Minnesota, a small farming town with a familiar language and unfamiliar opportunities.

He landed a job as a "cow tester" for Land O'Lakes, walking from farm to farm to inspect milk quality. He earned $70 a month, a sum he wore like a badge of honor. Within months, he had become deeply embedded in the local Danish community, attending church, joining the local theater, and living with a quiet sense of purpose.

Seven months later, he returned to Denmark, not to stay, but to marry his fiancée. A year after that, he had saved enough to pay for her voyage to America, this time with their infant daughter in her arms. A new life was taking root.

My father was born in Askov on July 22, 1932, one day after his twin brother. By then, my grandparents had five children, four of them born on American soil. But the timing was brutal. The Great Depression had reached Askov, bringing financial ruin. My grandfather had built a modest farm with five cows and a few livestock. By 1932, that dream collapsed. He lost nearly everything.

In a series of letters from my great-grandmother, it's clear she feared for the family's future in America. She urged him to return to Denmark, to regroup, and to survive. He took $350, no small sum at the time, and booked passage home. It couldn't have been an easy decision, leaving behind the country he had longed to make his own. But he didn't return defeated. He returned determined.

He didn't speak much about those years, but his actions told the story. He endured the German occupation of Denmark when Nazi forces invaded in 1940. He protected his family, kept them fed, and faced uncertainty with the same quiet resolve that carried him across the Atlantic in the first place.

That resilience didn't begin in America. It had been forged long before, during his childhood in Germany, where his father, my great-grandfather, served as Consular Secretary at the Danish Consulate in Frankfurt from 1897 to 1910. When my great-grandfather died, my grandfather was just nine years old, the youngest of three surviving children. His older brother later died at just nineteen.

Loss was nothing new to him.

But neither was persistence.

His motivation to pursue a better life wasn't born of comfort. It was born of hardship. America didn't give him that strength; it revealed it!

My grandfather rarely spoke of the past. He didn't romanticize the struggle or dwell on what might have been. He kept his eyes on the future and his feet firmly planted on the ground, taking responsibility for his actions. For the rest of his life, he remained focused on one thing: providing safety and stability for his family.

Though often soft-spoken, he commanded deep respect as our family's patriarch. Life had carved a pragmatic edge into him, a certain toughness that never overshadowed the warmth in the letters he had once written to his mother while in Askov. Those letters revealed a tender man who believed in love, community, and doing what was right, even when it was hard.

His story is a reminder that defeat is never final. He may have returned from America without riches, but not without purpose. *His legacy wasn't built on comfort; it was built on resilience.*

That's the essence of the American Dream.

And that's the immigrant spirit.

So the question isn't whether you'll face adversity, because you will.

The real question is: what will you build with it?

For me, the answer began in the most unglamorous way possible, with tiny wins. In sales, every order felt like a foothold, every display a chance to prove what was possible. Those small beginnings became the foundation of bigger outcomes, and they taught me that growth is rarely sudden. It is built one step, one relationship, one act of persistence at a time.

CHAPTER 5

Immigration Policy

Big victories are nothing more than small victories stacked over time.

Growing up in sales, I quickly learned that every sale was the beginning of the next one. It wasn't just about closing a deal; it was about growing myself, my abilities, and my relevance to others.

In my early days of selling furniture, when I was traveling around the country recruiting new dealers, my first goal was simple: get them to buy just enough to showcase the furniture on their floor. To help, I would assemble the pieces myself and support them with promotional literature from Denmark.

Each order was small, but each was a step forward. Every square foot of floor space mattered. Every display became a building block. These weren't just transactions; they were opportunities, each one an open lane to growth.

What I learned in sales also holds for nations: growth is never sudden; **it is built one step at a time**. Immigration works the same way.

Immigration is one of the most polarizing issues in American politics today, bouncing back and forth like a political football, used to rally crowds, score points, and win elections. But immigration is not a game. It is deeply personal. It shapes lives, families, economies, and the very soul of our nation. As an immigrant myself, I have lived both the challenges and the promise, and I've seen how policy debates often overlook the human reality at their core.

The Reality Behind the Rhetoric

Politics thrives on extremes, either opening the gates to everyone or closing the doors entirely. But the truth is more nuanced. **Immigration policy shouldn't be about pandering to fear or idealism; it should be about building a system that is rigorous, fair, transparent, and deeply aware of its economic and human impact.** For instance, immigrants make significant contributions to our healthcare system, including many who work as doctors and scientists. They also bring diverse perspectives and cultural richness, enriching our society.

Consider this: a 2022 study by Stuart Anderson of the National Foundation for American Policy found that **immigrants founded or co-founded 319 of the 582 U.S. startups valued at $1 billion or more**. Nearly half arrived in America as international students.

I was once one of those international students. Decades later, the data points show what I experienced firsthand: that students who come here often stay, innovate, and build companies that employ thousands.

This isn't just a statistic; it's proof that immigration fuels innovation, job creation, and global competitiveness. It's a testament to the potential and the economic growth that immigration can bring to our nation.

Debunking the Myths

The myth that immigrants "steal jobs" persists, but it ignores reality. Immigrants often take the jobs that are hardest to fill, the ones that demand resilience, sacrifice, and an openness to start over. These individuals aren't drains on the system; they are contributors. They are the people willing to build from nothing, a trait every entrepreneur should recognize and respect.

The United States, at its best, has always been a nation of arrivals. Yet, the portrayal of immigrants shifts with the political winds; they are heroes one decade and scapegoats the next. When expedience overrides principle, we all lose. A country built on freedom and opportunity cannot afford to treat immigration as a wedge issue without eroding its foundation. Immigrants are not just a part of our nation's history; they are the embodiment of the American Dream, striving for a better life and making significant contributions to our country's growth and prosperity.

Immigration as a Growth Strategy

We stand on the edge of another economic expansion. As industries reshore manufacturing and rebuild their supply chains, we will need skilled labor—and a lot of it. A balanced immigration system can meet this need without overburdening resources. The alternative is to repeat past mistakes, where immigrants were exploited as cheap labor, denied rights, and stripped of dignity.

Ethical immigration policy isn't just about economics; it's about moral leadership.

It's about ensuring that those who come here to contribute have the opportunity to do so within a system that protects their rights and rewards their efforts. It's about upholding our values and treating every individual with dignity and respect, regardless of their origin.

The Power of Exchange

One of the most promising tools we have is student exchange programs. These aren't just academic opportunities; they're bridges between cultures. For international students, it's a front-row seat to the American Experiment: its challenges, its freedoms, and its potential. For us, it's a chance to showcase our values beyond headlines and politics.

When students return home, or choose to stay, they carry with them a nuanced, lived understanding of what America represents. This type of cultural exchange is equally valuable for our young people. Nothing dismantles prejudice faster than genuine friendship across cultures.

Tying It Back to the Journey

Immigration is about more than borders and policy; it's about people.

It's about talent, potential, and the willingness to start from zero. For entrepreneurs, it's a familiar story: arriving in a new space, facing uncertainty, learning the rules, and finding ways to make a meaningful contribution.

Just as strong alliances fuel business growth, and conflict resolution keeps partnerships intact, a thoughtful immigration system fuels national growth and strengthens our collective future. If we steward immigration as the gift it can be, we won't just preserve the American Dream. We'll expand it to make it more inclusive, innovative, and resilient for generations to come.

But sometimes, life doesn't just hand you minor setbacks to overcome; it forces you to start over entirely. That's where the real test begins.

Before moving forward, I would like to pause and address some common misconceptions that often cloud the immigration debate. These distinctions matter not just in policy but also in how we understand fairness and opportunity.

Points of Clarification

In today's world of mass migration, the distinction between immigrants and refugees is often blurred. Refugee or asylum seeker status was designed to protect people in extraordinary crises: those escaping war, persecution, or natural disaster. However, over time, it has sometimes been used as a shortcut to circumvent established immigration processes. This creates tension: individuals who follow the rules and wait patiently in line may be pushed back by others who qualify under looser criteria.

Better Narrative Required

We have difficulty defining the various categories of people seeking to come to our country.

We have institutionalized legal and illegal Immigration. In my mind, there is no such thing as illegal immigration; instead, there is migration. Migration, by definition, refers to the voluntary movement of people within their own country or internationally, not as part of a process but through voluntary relocation. We have a problem with migration, not Illegal immigration, by definition. The term "illegal aliens" continues to define those who manage to violate our laws to enter our country illegally.

It would be much clearer if we were more disciplined in the characterization, making it absolutely clear that one has nothing to do with the other.

We do not have a method to accept migrants outside the process outlined in our immigration law. Migration, by definition, becomes more akin to squatters' rights than immigration, when borders are crossed without following the law.

Whenever we fail to clearly point out differences in easy-to-understand terms, we do everyone a huge disservice.

Another fact that seems poorly understood and articulated is that our foreign embassies and consulates the world over, for years, have been the designated recipients for migrants seeking to file an immigration petition. We are not receiving migrants on U.S. soil to be processed, on Ellis Island or at the border, and either admitted or sent back. In fact, we now require tourist visas to be issued overseas before departure to the U.S.

Immigration is not charity; it is an opportunity.

A firm and fair system should benchmark refugee protections against the actual conditions in a person's country of origin, not simply the disparity between their quality of life and ours. When the lines are blurred, the system begins to lose integrity, and the people who could contribute most may be left waiting.

This does not mean closing our doors to those in desperate need. **On the contrary, it means ensuring that compassion is targeted where it is most justified, while also protecting the fairness of the process.** Refugees deserve dignity, but so do immigrants who commit to the long path of qualification and contribution.

When distinctions collapse, the results are damaging for everyone. Communities lose trust in the system, resentment grows, and exploitation takes root. Worse still, vulnerable migrants become easy targets for cartels and criminal networks that promise protection but deliver only exploitation and despair.

A thoughtful immigration policy must strike a balance between opportunity and order, compassion and clarity. Immigrants should be evaluated on their merit, character, skills, and family ties, not on loopholes or financial shortcuts. Refugees should continue to find safety here, but not at the expense of those who follow the legal process.

If we fail to maintain this balance, we create fertile ground for division and distrust. If we succeed, we preserve both the generosity and the integrity of our nation, ensuring that immigration remains not just a doorway of entry, but a pathway to contribution, growth, and shared prosperity.

CHAPTER 6

Learning Beyond the Classroom

The whole learning bit is a lifelong journey. It's something you do every day, and that shapes your perspective.

In my early school years, I struggled, not because of a lack of intelligence, but because I couldn't connect the dots. I couldn't see the relevance. I didn't understand why we were learning what we were learning. And when a kid doesn't understand *why*, it's hard to expect them to care about *how*. For years, I was labeled a poor student. Not because I couldn't learn, but because no one explained *why* it mattered.

And so, I sat in school, staring out the window, wondering why I was there and what the point of the lesson plan even was. None of it connected to me or my life. The teacher's words blurred into the background like static, and my mind wandered to the one thing that challenged my mind and made sense: building Lego trains.

I could almost feel the smooth plastic pieces in my hands and hear the satisfying click as they snapped into place. I'd imagine designing the perfect locomotive, one that was longer, faster, and unstoppable. I'd picture it gliding effortlessly through sharp turns, staying steady on the track no matter how tight the curve. That daydream was my escape, my little spark of creativity in a world that felt otherwise dull and confining.

By seventh grade, a judgment was made for each student in Denmark: are you destined for trade school or university? After a PTA meeting, my father came home and said, "The principal doesn't think you're going to amount to anything that has anything to do with using your head." It wasn't meant to be cruel; it was just how the system operated and had become standard practice. But my dad, a carpenter, looked at me and said, "There's no shame in being a tradesman. But I think you're smarter than that. I believe in you."

My father's belief in me, spoken at a time when others did not recognize my potential and had essentially written me off, sparked something deep within my soul. His words and belief in me changed how I saw myself and ultimately the course of my life. I was proud of my dad and of his being a skilled tradesman, but I knew I wasn't meant for that line of work or the lifestyle. I knew my brain worked differently, my skill set lay in other areas, and that I was naturally drawn to business-minded things: finding opportunities, solving problems, and building something from the ground up. I realized I had a passion for strategy, innovation, and taking calculated risks to create something meaningful. His support was a crucial factor in my journey of self-discovery and personal growth.

My father's words filled me with determination to reach my potential, chase my dreams, and succeed. I worked hard, caught up to my peers, including those with the highest marks, and moved from the trade school track to the university path. Along the way, I rose to the position of student council president, led major projects, and ultimately became the only student in my graduating class to earn a scholarship to study abroad in the United States. In doing so, I proved not only to myself but also to those who once doubted and dismissed me that I was capable of much more.

That was when I learned I could earn victories, that this was my victory. I didn't do it for anyone else. I did it for me.

The Power of a Blank Slate

Earning a scholarship to study in the U.S. was a dream come true, but it was only the beginning of an incredible journey. Stepping off the plane as an exchange student, with just a suitcase in hand and a mix of nerves and excitement, I found myself entering an entirely new world full of possibilities.

Back home, I always felt trapped, boxed in by expectations I never agreed to, labeled in ways I never chose, and surrounded by people who thought they had me all figured out.

First, "the quiet one," then the "outspoken one" and "a dreamer." You know the drill; we all get labeled as children and carry those labels with us, like a sign around our necks, into our teenage years and often into adulthood. The labels around me had stuck early on, no matter what I did to try to break free. And it was suffocating. High school had been the first step toward personal liberation, but I was still stuck in a culture that did not encourage me to break the norms. Every step I took felt weighed down by this invisible pressure to be what everyone else thought I was supposed to be.

But here?

Here, everything was different.

I was a blank slate, no labels, no judgments, no one telling me what I could or couldn't achieve. For once, people were genuinely curious, interested in me, not because of some role I'd been shoved into, but simply because I was me. For the first time in what felt like forever, I could breathe. I could dream bigger, explore who I was, and leave behind all the restrictions I hadn't even realized I'd been living under.

Can you relate to that? Have you ever felt like your identity was reduced to a single label, like being "the class clown" or something else that didn't wholly define you?

It's exhausting, isn't it?

But breaking free of those labels?

That feeling is pure liberation! It's a step toward embracing your true self, unencumbered by others' expectations.

My newfound sense of freedom opened my eyes to new possibilities. I realized I didn't have to fit a mold and could redefine myself entirely based on *who I wanted to be*. For the first time in my life, that idea felt exhilarating rather than terrifying. Not through reinvention, but through effort, openness, and persistence. And I learned a crucial truth:

It doesn't matter what your history is.
Your defeats don't define you; they inform you.

That's what true education is.

True education *is not* about sitting quietly in a classroom, memorizing dates in history, or even solving algebraic equations. It's about understanding the why behind these lessons, their importance, and how they can be applied to our lives in the future. This understanding is what truly engages us in the learning process.

As a young student, I was disengaged and uninterested in learning because I was essentially told to learn for the sake of it, but I wanted to understand the purpose behind it all. Over the years, I've learned that true education is about more than just acquiring knowledge. It's about developing critical thinking, resilience in the face of challenges, and the ability to see opportunities where others see obstacles. It's also about fostering creativity, adaptability, and a lifelong curiosity for learning. Schools can hand you tools, but only you can decide what to build with them.

That's why it's important to distinguish between education and formal schooling. For example, in the United States, we're frequently introduced by a title, lead with our credentials, and proudly hang our degrees on the walls. While there's nothing inherently wrong with celebrating academic achievements, we sometimes assign too much value to them. A degree or title doesn't automatically mean someone is capable or has practical, real-world knowledge.

I've known plenty of people who could ace an exam but struggled to solve real-life problems. They could recite theories word for word but couldn't apply them when it mattered, when the rubber met the road. True intelligence and ability go beyond what's written on a diploma—they're demonstrated by action, adaptability, and the ability to think critically under real-world conditions.

They couldn't put all the tools in the toolbox together and use them constructively.

In Denmark and much of Europe, your credentials define your future. Without the right qualifications, your skills and experience are often overlooked. If I hadn't been switched to the university track, I would have been forced to learn a trade instead. And even if I had spent 15 years mastering that trade, I'd only be able to work if I held the proper credentials. Without a diploma or formal certification, your experience doesn't count.

Simply put: No diploma? No opportunity.

The United States, in contrast, has long symbolized the American Dream: the idea that anyone, regardless of their background, can achieve success through hard work and determination. It offered something unique: the freedom to prove yourself. You didn't need permission to take a risk or chase a goal; you just needed grit and the belief that effort and perseverance could turn ambition into reality.

If you had a bad chapter, okay. How does that inform the next chapter? It doesn't define you. It's just what happened.

And yet, I see too many people, especially the young, treat mistakes as if they're permanent, as if one wrong decision is a life sentence. Whether it's choosing the "wrong" major, taking a job that doesn't work out, or making a bad call in a relationship, they carry the weight of these choices as if they can't recover. However, the truth is that mistakes are often just stepping stones, teaching us lessons we need to learn to grow and move forward. You can start over again as many times as required.

Learning isn't linear. It's not about staying on track; it's about *staying in motion.*

We have this fascination with the idea that we're on a life track and that once we reach a certain age, we can no longer do certain things. Come on. If you feel up to it, *do it*.

Starting over takes humility, courage, and risk.

However, risk is not something to fear; it's something to embrace, especially when chasing something meaningful. We all make mistakes;

it's part of being human. But mistakes don't have to be the end of the road. They're opportunities to learn and grow. The difference lies in realizing that missteps are just detours, not dead ends. Starting fresh is proof that you're willing to turn mistakes into new beginnings.

> **Risk is at the very core of it. If you want to be an entrepreneur, you have to love risk more than anything in the world. It's not logical. People will ask, "Why would you do that?" But that's exactly why you *must* do it.**

The truth is, we live in a world that's becoming more risk-averse. We outsource risk to the government, to the rich, or to those who "have it all figured out," expecting them to shoulder the responsibility. We look for guarantees at every turn, whether it's in our careers, relationships, or decisions. But here's the thing: you can't grow if you're unwilling to take risks.

Growth comes from stepping into the unknown, even when it's uncomfortable. And you can't truly learn if you don't take the time to reflect, whether it's on mistakes, successes, or the choices that scare you the most.

> **Real progress means embracing both risk and reflection. If you don't reflect, then you don't learn. If you make a mistake and don't reflect on it, how did you learn anything?**

We wrap ourselves in the patchwork quilt of our past, each square telling its own story. A failed marriage stitched with heartache and broken vows, a bad grade sewn in with threads of regret and self-doubt. There's the harsh fabric of bankruptcy, frayed at the edges, a reminder of dreams that unraveled. Each patch lingers, carrying the weight of mistakes, missed chances, and the haunting whispers of what-ifs.

Each piece is stitched together with threads of regret and self-doubt, creating a heavy weight that feels almost comforting in its familiarity. We convince ourselves it's safer to stay warm beneath it, cocooned in what we know, still carrying our old labels, rather than risk the chill of stepping out, embracing who we truly are, and trying again.

"What if my idea doesn't work?"

"What if I stumble once more?"

"What if I fail again?"

"What if?"

Starting over can feel overwhelming, like facing an endless winter storm. You've just finished shoveling the driveway, your breath visible in the icy air, muscles aching from the effort, only for the snow to start falling again, thick and relentless. It's exhausting, frustrating, and tempting to give up. But starting over, like confronting that storm, takes courage. Each scoop of snow, each step forward, brings you closer to clearing the way.

The storm will pass, and the driveway will be clear. Often, though, we stay put, burdened by fear, convincing ourselves it's safer to endure the familiar than face the unknown. Yet deep down, a quiet voice wonders: What if trying again doesn't bring more cold but instead a warmth we've never imagined?

Don't keep wearing the damn blanket. Hang it on the wall and ask yourself: what's the *next* patch you want to sew into it?

Education isn't just what you did in the past; it's what you choose to do *now!* It's not limited to a classroom, a phase of life, or the numbers on a diploma. Education is a lifelong journey, constantly evolving and growing with you. It's alive and ongoing, belonging to those who embrace it with curiosity, courage, and a drive to keep learning, no matter where they are in life.

So, whether you're a student, an entrepreneur, or someone still figuring it out, know that you are not the sum of your grades. You are not your past chapter. You are what you choose to learn next.

CHAPTER 7

Challenge and Response

A Fork in the Road

What came next was proof of the lesson I had just learned: life's most significant challenges often arrive disguised as endings. When we lose something we've poured ourselves into, something built with sacrifice, conviction, and passion, the loss feels devastating. Yet it is in those moments that we're given the chance to choose: cling to what no longer fits, or step forward into what's next.

By 2001, I had spent years pouring myself into work, giving days, nights, and weekends to help turn a struggling subsidiary of a Fortune 200 company into a success. As an immigrant who had worked his way up to director, I took pride in what we had accomplished. But over time, it became clear that the way we approached challenges and the solutions we believed in no longer resonated with our corporate masters.

The final signal came when I found myself across the table from a newly appointed president. The very position had once been held up as an incentive for me, a reward for loyalty and results. Yet now it belonged to someone who hadn't invested a single hour in the battles we had fought or the victories we had earned. Despite the turnaround I had helped lead, they judged that I had "fallen short on decorum." The message was clear: my time in that chapter was drawing to a close.

When I was presented with three untenable options for continuing my career, clarity replaced doubt. I picked up my briefcase, looked my new boss in the eye, and resigned on the spot. I had no safety net, no mapped-out plan. But I had thought enough about what might come next to know that I would rather walk into uncertainty on my terms than compromise my values for the illusion of security. The strength to pursue the next chapter came directly from the decision to close the prior one.

That moment taught me an enduring lesson: sometimes the destiny we think we want is not truly ours if it requires us to abandon our principles. What felt like an ending was, in fact, a fork in the road that led to far greater things than I could see at the time.

The courage to close one chapter is what gives you the strength to begin the next.

And that's the point of this chapter. **Challenges aren't confined to careers, or even to one country; they are universal.** And nowhere is that more evident than in the journey of an immigrant.

The Immigrant's Challenge

From money to marriage to health, challenges come to us in every season of life. For immigrants, those challenges are magnified. Starting over in a new country demands adaptation at every level: language, culture, community, and career. What once felt familiar is suddenly foreign, and the only way forward is to learn, adjust, and grow faster than you thought possible.

It doesn't matter whether you arrive as a seasonal worker, with little more than hope, or as a highly trained professional with years of expertise; adversity will still find you. Skills alone don't guarantee success. You must bridge the gap between what you know and what you need to learn, between the world you left behind and the one you've entered.

Adversity doesn't discriminate.

It visits everyone.

What matters is how you respond.

This process isn't easy. It demands resilience, humility, and persistence. There are times when setbacks feel fundamental, when the bank account is empty, the marriage feels strained, or the body gives out under stress. In those moments, motivation doesn't come from pep talks or optimism. It comes from sheer necessity. You push forward because stopping simply isn't an option.

The Power of Community

But success doesn't come from grit alone.

You cannot thrive in isolation.

To truly integrate, you must also become part of your new community, finding friends, mentors, and associates who can help you understand and appreciate the differences. Without connection, the road becomes lonely, and opportunities remain scarce. With it, doors begin to open.

Resilience will get you started.

Relationships will carry you through.

The immigrants who succeed are the ones who combine persistence with adaptability. They accept that setbacks are part of the story but refuse to let those setbacks define them. They are willing to ask for help, build relationships, and contribute to their new environment, rather than standing apart from it. Community is not just support—it's an opportunity multiplier.

Lessons Beyond Immigration

And here's the larger lesson: the immigrant's story is also the entrepreneur's story. At their core, both journeys are about risk, resilience, and reinvention.

When you start something new, whether it's a business, a career, or a life in another country, you will face resistance, uncertainty, and moments when failure feels inevitable. But if you keep moving forward, if you're willing to learn from others, and if you see challenges not as punishments but as invitations to grow, then those very obstacles become your advantage.

Every setback carries a seed of progress, if you're willing to plant it.

Adversity is not the end of the story; it is the raw material from which success is built.

The real question isn't whether you'll encounter adversity, but, when you face it, what will you build with it?

For me, the answer began in the most unassuming of places, on showroom floors across the Midwest, where every small victory laid the foundation for much larger outcomes.

CHAPTER 8

Expectations and Outcomes

The Power of Small Beginnings

"Celebrate the first step; it's the beginning of something greater."

As a young salesperson, I was eager to learn and grow. I quickly realized that every sale was not just a transaction, but the beginning of a new relationship.

Each order was small, but each was a step forward. Every square foot of floor space mattered. Every display became a building block. These weren't just sales; they were opportunities, the seeds of growth that would one day expand far beyond what I could see at the time.

Each step forward is not just about revenue; it's about growth, in your abilities, authenticity, and relevance to others.

In my early days of selling furniture, traveling around the Midwest to recruit new dealers, the first goal was simple: get them to buy just enough to showcase our Danish pieces on the floor. We supported them with promotional literature from Denmark, often delivering and assembling the furniture myself, Danish "IKEA-style" kits that I lugged, bolted, and polished until they stood proudly in a showroom. Those initial orders weren't large, but they were symbolic. Every square foot of floor space was a foothold, every display a doorway to greater opportunity.

Working for a small salary with the hope of great returns, I was motivated more by the possibility than the paychecks. One store at a time, we expanded our dealership network from just three shops to a presence in nearly every city in the Midwest with a population of more than 50,000.

Each success, no matter how small, was a testament to our perseverance and determination. And these small victories built the momentum we needed to keep moving forward.

Persistence in Long Journeys

That same principle carried into my parking meter career. Selling to municipalities was no small task. The cycle spanned 18 to 36 months, encompassing requirements, development, politics, and public bidding.

Success didn't come overnight, so *we broke the process into smaller wins*: marketing milestones, product refinements, and community outreach.

We celebrated every achievement, no matter how small.

A new software feature was completed. A pilot project was launched. A city official said, "I'll hear you out." Each was a spark of progress, proof that we were moving forward. Over time, these sparks ignited transformation, not just of our company but of an entire industry.

Big victories are made from a thousand small ones strung together.

Expectations Shape Outcomes

This mindset of celebrating incremental progress is the same one that drives successful immigrants. Immigrants rarely arrive expecting ease. Most come with realistic expectations: that they will start at the bottom, face hardship, and climb slowly, step by step. They know risk is the entry fee, and they embrace it.

Throughout history, this has been the story of immigrants. The Irish, arriving after the Great Famine, took up arms in the Civil War, driven by the promise of pay and citizenship. The Chinese laborers who carved railroads through mountains and deserts helped bind America together from coast to coast. These men and women carried burdens most people today can scarcely imagine, but they kept moving forward.

The same principle applies now as it did then: expectations define outcomes. Those who see hardship as part of the journey endure. Those who set milestones, celebrating small victories instead of chasing instant gratification, stay motivated long enough to build something lasting.

Set your expectations as milestones, not finish lines.

Building Beyond Survival

At my company, Tuxen & Associates, Inc., which has been in business for twenty-five years, I've carried this lesson forward. Every client interaction, every sale, every new opportunity is cause for recognition. Today, some of my greatest joy comes not from my wins but from celebrating my team's accomplishments and growth. Their victories are the continuation of a journey that began when I carried Danish furniture into American showrooms.

The immigrant's experience teaches us that embracing challenges has rewards. The entrepreneur's journey teaches the same. Success is not born in leaps; it is built in layers, stitched together by perseverance, relationships, and perspective.

And so, whether you are new to a country, an industry, or a dream, remember this: adversity will meet you. But if you carry realistic expectations, measure progress step by step, and celebrate the victories along the way, your outcomes will not only sustain you, but they will also multiply into something greater than you imagined.

CHAPTER 9

Building Beyond the Blueprint

Product Development: A Case Study in Best Practices

Throughout my career, I have worked with and represented manufacturing companies, helping them develop truly customer-centric businesses, products, and solutions. My role in understanding and addressing customer needs has been pivotal in this process.

That work has ranged from furniture design to electronics hardware development and software integration. While numerous examples exist, this chapter will focus on one: the creation of the next-generation parking meter and its integrated software management system. It was my first large-scale project and, by far, the most challenging. We had to learn everything from scratch, including how to approach product development itself.

Every product journey is different, depending on the industry and offering. Yet the process is universal: research, strategy, design, development, launch, and iteration. Familiarity with the process can provide a sense of comfort as you navigate the product development journey.

1. Ideation & Discovery

Product development begins not with a solution, but with a problem. You must thoroughly understand customer pain points, validate demand through research, and clearly define your target audience. Cross-functional brainstorming is crucial; all key stakeholders, including engineering, marketing, design, and customer support, should be at the table from the outset.

In the mid-1980s, Duncan Industries introduced the world's first electronic parking meter, replacing mechanical components with electronic ones. It was revolutionary: accurate digital timekeeping, remote programming, and operations data. Dover Corporation acquired Duncan, banking on its potential.

But they missed something critical. The very data-collection features touted as progress created resistance among those responsible for collecting money. Accountability was being introduced, and it clashed with the existing culture.

I undertook both internal studies and field interviews with major customers. What I found was simple but profound: the manufacturer's expectations and the customer's needs did not align.

At that time, I had just been promoted to Director of Business Development and Engineering after serving as Vice President of Duncan Management Solutions, our software joint venture. In this role, I was responsible for identifying new business opportunities, building strategic partnerships, and aligning our product development with market needs. My experience reengineering our enforcement platform into a broader management solution provided me with a unique perspective on how hardware and software must work together to meet real customer needs.

It became clear that the sales proposition for the hardware alone would never succeed. We had to offer a fully integrated management system, a paradigm shift in how on-street parking was managed.

2. Planning & Strategy

A clear product vision was essential. We aligned around measurable objectives and defined outcomes before designing solutions. Using Quality Function Deployment (QFD), we ensured alignment with the needs articulated by our stakeholders.

We also adopted what is now known as the OKR framework, comprising Objectives and Key Results, long before it became mainstream. Our goal was ambitious: to deliver a fully integrated solution without incurring heavy, non-recurring engineering expenses, thereby avoiding the need to return to our corporate masters for funding during a turnaround.

Strategic alliances with key industry players, combined with disciplined planning, made this possible. We leveraged the expertise of our engineering partners at Duncan Industries and in software at Duncan Management Solutions, ensuring they worked hand in hand to build a seamless, end-to-end system. Our meticulous planning, covering every aspect of the project from design to launch, ensured we stayed on track and met our objectives.

3. Design & Prototyping

Time was of the essence. Specifications were shaped in close collaboration with the target cities, and we knew that being first to market would define the industry standard. The urgency and excitement in rapid prototyping should be palpable in the product development journey.

We focused on rapid prototyping, scalability, and flexibility, anticipating needs that customers had not yet articulated.

4. Development

Building the new parking meter required reengineering every electronic component and its housing. Traditionally, housings were cast in zinc, a process that was both expensive and time-consuming. Each mold cost $175,000 and required up to eight months to complete.

Then New York City issued a request for proposal, demanding fully functional prototypes within 90 days. We faced an impossible challenge: the electronics could be ready, but the housings could not.

We turned to an emerging technology: 3D laser printing. At the time, it was unproven for production, but it allowed us to quickly create interim molds. Those molds produced enough housings to deliver prototypes on time.

5. Launch

Through an all-hands effort, we delivered 25 prototypes to New York City, meeting their deadline. The risk paid off: we won an order for 15,000 meters and included our integrated software platform in the contract.

The launch redefined our marketing strategy and repositioned us in the marketplace. Soon, Washington, DC and Los Angeles followed, and within a few years, integrated management systems became the global standard for on-street parking.

6. Post-Launch & Iteration

Product development does not end at launch. It requires measurement, customer feedback, and continuous improvement. Our initial rollouts faced challenges, particularly in the user interface and payment processing. However, by responding quickly, owning the problems, and supporting customers in real-time, we turned setbacks into trust. We made significant improvements based on customer feedback, enhancing the user interface and streamlining the payment process, thereby boosting customer satisfaction.

Ultimately, the actual test of a product is not whether it works perfectly on Day 1, but whether customers believe you'll stand with them on Day 1000.

Cultural Foundations

None of this would have been possible without cultural change inside the company. Our president took a bet not just on technology, but also on people. He entrusted me with leading teams to collaborate across silos and empowered us to take risks. Culture and product development were inseparable; one could not succeed without the other.

Growth is never just about numbers on a page; it's about people, their potential, their development, and their willingness to grow alongside you. When you invest in people, you create value that lasts far beyond any single venture.

And that investment in people is most powerful when it's authentic. In an age increasingly shaped by screens and filters, I've learned that nothing replaces real presence. That's where the next chapter begins.

CHAPTER 10

Work Versus Play and Fulfillment

For most of us, work is something we were told we have to do, a path laid out by society that we often follow without question. We wake up to the blare of an alarm clock, groaning as we wipe the sleep from our eyes. The coffee machine whirs as we move through the motions on autopilot, pouring the first cup of caffeine just to feel human. We scroll through our phones, half-reading emails or social media updates, dreading the day ahead. Then we hop into our cars, merging into the same gridlocked traffic as yesterday, barely paying attention to the road as our minds drift. By the time we park, we can't even remember the drive.

Once at work, the day becomes a blur of meetings that seem to go in circles, emails that pile up faster than we can respond, and tasks that feel repetitive and unimportant. Lunch is often eaten at our desks, scrolling through more screens to distract ourselves from the monotony. There's little satisfaction in the work we're doing, as the hours drag on and tasks increasingly feel like checking boxes rather than making a meaningful impact.

We glance at the clock, watching the minutes tick by until it's finally time to punch out. Exhausted, we head home, too drained to pursue hobbies or spend quality time with loved ones. The cycle repeats the next day: the same alarm, the same commute, the same routine. Yet we continue, dragging ourselves back to the grind, wondering if this is all there is, but feeling stuck in the loop.

It's routine; it's expected; but is it fulfilling?

What if work could be more than just going through the motions?

What if it could be something that brings pride, purpose, and real meaning to our days?

It all begins with understanding what genuinely fulfills you and what you excel at. When you can identify your core attributes, natural talents, and personal values, you can build a path that feels less like a grind and more like a calling. Creating a list of what gives you energy, what challenges you in the right way, and what makes you feel alive can be a powerful compass. It doesn't just guide your career; it shapes your identity.

I've often admired tradespeople, such as carpenters, mechanics, and masons, who can stand back after a long day and see exactly what they've created. The satisfaction of a job well done is immediate, tangible, and deeply gratifying. That sense of pride doesn't rely on applause or external validation. It lives in the quiet moment when you say to yourself, "I did that."

Relevance isn't a luxury. It's a basic human need. We all long to matter, to know that what we do makes a difference. Building confidence comes from understanding how to create results, recognizing them, and taking pride in them. Even small victories, such as completing a task, earning trust, or making someone's day better, build a track record of purpose. These seemingly minor moments become touchstones in seasons when progress feels invisible.

Failure, too, has its place. It is not a dead end but part of the curriculum. There is no real learning without it. When you're in the valley, it can feel hollow to say, "Failure is a gift," but if you take inventory of the lessons learned, you'll realize failure teaches more than success ever could. The story you tell yourself about failure will shape how you show up the next time around.

Nowhere is this more relevant than in the world of entrepreneurship. Starting something from nothing requires you to become intimately familiar with trial and error. Entrepreneurship, at its core, is a series of experiments. You make a thousand decisions with incomplete information and hope you learn fast enough to stay in the game. Success isn't about avoiding failure; it's about being resilient enough to extract meaning from it.

This is a stark contrast to many traditional jobs where the risks are managed by someone else. You might get a bonus, a promotion, or even face termination, but your livelihood isn't tethered to every decision. Entrepreneurs eat what they kill. It's not for everyone.

You have to love the hunt, not just the feast. If the process doesn't excite you more than the outcome, entrepreneurship might feel like a burden. But if it does excite you, if waking up to uncertainty stirs something in you, then you're not working in the traditional sense. You're playing. You're building something that doesn't just feed your family but also feeds your soul.

The most successful entrepreneurs aren't chasing money. They're chasing relevance. They want to know that their work matters, that it impacts others, and that it endures beyond their lifetime. They derive fulfillment not from recognition but from knowing that their ideas and efforts have created something valuable and meaningful for others.

But this pursuit of purpose isn't just for entrepreneurs. Everyone, regardless of their role, deserves the opportunity to step back and assess their impact. Whether you're a teacher, a nurse, a chef, a manager, or a stay-at-home parent, fulfillment comes not from the size of the task but from the heart you bring to it. It's about contribution, not compensation.

Too often today, entrepreneurship is romanticized as creating hype and securing investors. But real entrepreneurship is proving your idea in the fire of reality. It's not about how impressive your pitch deck looks; it's about whether you've built something that works, something that solves a real problem, something you can be proud of.

In a world where there's more money chasing ideas than there are ideas worth chasing, it's tempting to follow the money. But if you haven't done the work, if you can't step back and feel proud of what you've created, no dollar amount will satisfy that inner void.

The truth is this: if the process does not fulfill you, you'll always be searching for the next high. But if you can love the journey, celebrate small wins, learn from setbacks, and keep showing up, you'll discover that work is no longer just work. It's a calling. And relevance will follow.

CHAPTER 11

Virtualism vs. Realism

In a world where filters often obscure reality, the unique perspective of immigrants shines through. This chapter explores their innate tendency to value authenticity, a trait that fosters deeper trust in both business and personal life.

The immigrant journey has always been rooted in learning and education. You arrive in a new land with limited tools, uncertain opportunities, and the daunting task of starting over. Over the past four decades, technology has provided incredible resources for learning; however, it remains only a tool. It cannot shake a hand, build trust, or replace the human bonds that ultimately determine success.

As an immigrant, you are often met with both curiosity and skepticism. Language becomes the first test. If you cannot communicate fluently, it is harder to establish credibility with those around you. Written communication can be an even steeper climb. But while language skills are crucial, they are not the full measure of trust. **What bridges the gap is presence: your willingness to show up, sit across the table, and commit your time, talent, and treasure to a relationship.**

The Power of Presence

A personal encounter carries a weight that no virtual interaction can replicate. It's a potent signal of commitment, a *declaration that the relationship matters enough for a physical presence.* In business, this presence is a tangible demonstration of investment in the relationship, not just the transaction. Conversations that extend beyond the deal itself, touching on the person in front of you, create a foundation that no virtual platform can match.

I remember one of my earliest ventures in the United States, when I was trying to sell Scandinavian furniture. I didn't have a big marketing budget or a polished pitch deck. What I had was a willingness to show up. I drove long hours, set up pieces in dealer showrooms myself, and then stayed to talk with the owners, not just about the furniture, but about their families, their frustrations, and their hopes for their business. Those conversations built trust far more quickly than any glossy catalog ever could. The deals that followed weren't just about furniture; they were about relationships and the confidence those relationships fostered.

Sometimes that presence opened unexpected doors. On a sales trip to downtown Cleveland, I walked into a traditional furniture store and thought, "This will be a short visit." But the owner, a compassionate Jewish gentleman, asked if I was from Denmark. When I said yes, we began talking about the Danish Resistance during World War II and how they helped Jews escape to Sweden when Denmark could no longer shield them from the Nazis. By the end of that conversation, he signed on as a customer and, over time, became a good friend.

That lesson echoed the very heart of the immigrant journey: **risk is unavoidable, resilience is essential, but neither means much unless you're willing to be fully present. This resilience, this willingness to keep showing up, is a key factor in building trust.**

Trust isn't built through screens; it's built face-to-face, where presence proves commitment.

The Limits of the Virtual World

Even in an age of video conferencing and instant connection, the image on the screen often fails to reconcile with reality. Virtual interactions tend to accelerate timelines, narrowing conversations to outcomes rather than relationships. This makes it more challenging to establish trust at the outset of a journey.

Once trust is established, technology can be a valuable supplement to the process. Virtual tools can facilitate conversations, reduce travel, and expand reach. But as a starting point, they are poor substitutes for authenticity and realism. **Without presence, there is no depth, only noise.**

A Culture of Filters

The COVID era accelerated a shift toward what I call **synthetic reality**. Screens became mirrors, filled with whatever image we wanted to project, often polished, filtered, and detached from who we are.

But in this world of filters, **your authentic presence stands out**. It's a beacon of genuine connection in a sea of synthetic images. This authenticity is a powerful tool in a culture of filters, helping you stand out and build real connections.

In fact, the obsession with broadcasting, chasing views, likes, and impressions, mirrors the old Nielsen ratings in television. It measures reach, not relationship. And while reach may create attention, it does not build trust. *Genuine connection comes from meaningful engagement, not just numbers on a screen.*

Returning to What's Real

For immigrants, authenticity has always been the differentiator. You may stumble over words, but if your presence is genuine, your commitment clear, and your values lived out, people will lean in.

Authenticity outlasts filters.

Realism outshines noise.

In a world where synthetic images dominate, there is a tremendous opportunity to stand out by doing the countercultural thing: showing up, listening deeply, and building relationships face-to-face. *Business, like life, moves at the speed of trust, and trust only grows where authenticity is present.*

It is the same spirit that carried us through culture shock, from starting with nothing to chasing altitude one step at a time: **the willingness to show up, fully and authentically, no matter the risk.**

CHAPTER 12

The Pillars of Growth

Success, the type that lasts, doesn't come from shortcuts or dollar signs. It grows from character. Over the years, I've seen numerous examples, both inspiring and disappointing, of what happens when people confuse money with meaning or talent with teamwork. It's the character that truly defines a leader and inspires others to follow.

I've learned that three traits—**Attitude, Aptitude,** and **Altitude**—are key to success. These traits separate those who build something lasting from those who burn out chasing quick wins.

When Ethics Take a Back Seat

Today, it's easier than ever to lose your compass. Society equates success with wealth, rarely pausing to consider how that wealth was acquired or the consequences it left behind. Articles celebrate the young startup founder who raised millions in a single night. Investors rush in, convinced the idea will "obviously" take root in the market. Teams are hired like professional athletes, assembled quickly, bought for their skills, not their shared values.

But business is not an individual sport. Without shared character, ambition turns into conflict. Everyone chases personal wins while neglecting the very customers they are meant to serve. Before long, ethics becomes nothing more than a legal clause, poorly defined, inconsistently applied, and used more as a shield for investors than as a compass for leaders.

I've watched organizations twist themselves into knots trying to write ethics policies. But paper rules don't build character. People do. And if you don't trust your team to hold themselves accountable, you shouldn't have hired them in the first place.

Lead with Character

The apparent truth is also the most often overlooked: **lead with character and expect character in return.** Build consensus around shared values. *Put integrity at the top of the performance evaluation, above profit margins or market share.* When people are accountable to themselves, to their team, and to the mission, you don't need a thick manual of rules.

You need trust.

Over the years, I've distilled this principle into what I call the three pillars of personal growth:

Attitude.

Aptitude.

Altitude.

These aren't buzzwords.

They're habits of character that shape who you are, how you grow, and how far you go.

Attitude: The Foundation

Attitude defines your values, as well as those of the people around you. It's humility in practice, the willingness to serve others before serving yourself. It's believing that if you do right by others, they may do right by you, pressing forward even when they don't.

Attitude means not letting disappointment turn you into a bitter or cynical person. You keep walking your path, holding firm to your principles, trusting that those who cut corners will eventually face themselves in the mirror. Attitude is the quiet strength that enables you to keep showing up, even when others fall away.

Aptitude: The Work of Growth

Aptitude refers to your capacity to learn and your willingness to continue learning. It's curiosity paired with discipline, the practice of listening, questioning, and retesting what you think you know.

Real aptitude doesn't rest on yesterday's success. It analyzes, adapts, and applies lessons to tomorrow's challenges. It takes humility to admit you don't know everything and courage to keep testing your convictions. Aptitude is what keeps you moving forward when others grow complacent.

Altitude: The Reach of Ambition

Altitude is ambition, the drive to rise higher. But ambition without values is dangerous. Chasing money alone is empty. Altitude that matters is grounded in patience, discipline, and incremental victories.

It's the relentless pursuit of long-term goals, not the thrill of short-term wins. It's building brick by brick, climbing step by step, never abandoning your values for the sake of speed. True altitude is not measured in titles, earnings, or market share. It's measured in the distance you've traveled without betraying who you are.

The True Measure of Success

If these three traits: Attitude, Aptitude, and Altitude, define you and your team, you'll never need to worry about "policies on ethics." The definition will already be clear. Each person will know how to hold themselves accountable. Each will be invested in more than profit: in the authenticity of their work, in the trust of their peers, and in the growth of something larger than themselves.

Because at the end of the day, success isn't about how high you climb or how much you accumulate. It's about who you become along the way and whether the team beside you is growing with you.

"Character is the compass. Attitude, Aptitude, and Altitude are the path."

CHAPTER 13

Paying It Forward

Immigrants often lead with service. Mentorship, volunteering, and giving back aren't just nice gestures; they are essential ingredients for lasting success. Building something meaningful means lifting others as you climb. It's a lesson my father taught me early in life, one that has profoundly shaped the way I approach business decisions and entrepreneurship. He always emphasized the importance of giving back, showing me through his actions how service can create a lasting impact.

Lessons From My Father

My father started his spec home construction company with two partners in 1969. I was twelve years old. At the time, I hadn't realized that our family's standard of living had been scaled back when Dad left his secure job. Among the many casualties was his car; he traded his Audi for a 1950s vintage sedan that coughed and groaned down the road.

So I was surprised one day when the company acquired a brand-new Volvo station wagon. To my astonishment, Dad handed the keys over, not to himself, but to the company's first hire, a framing carpenter.

"Why does he get the new car when we're driving this old junker?" I asked.

Dad explained patiently, "Son, this gentleman has a family to feed, and he brings skills we need to build our company. We did not ask him to take the risk of starting this business—that risk belongs to my partners and me. We're the ones who chose this path, and it's our responsibility to take the hit if it fails."

That moment left a lasting imprint, etched deep with emotion I'll never forget.

My father always put people first, investing not only financially but also personally, in developing their potential and ensuring they thrived alongside him. His **actions** taught me that leadership isn't about being served but serving others. My father modeled authentic leadership and taught me that success is not measured by what you keep for yourself, but by *what you give and invest in others.*

During those early years working for him, I felt like I was the one taking the biggest risk. After all, I was earning minimum wage for work I believed was worth much more. But in hindsight, the real payoff wasn't the money; it was the mentoring. My father's example became a living lesson that hard work and guidance multiply in ways far greater than a paycheck.

Mentorship, Motivation, and Mutual Success

Those early lessons shaped the way I built my businesses. I came to see that **building talent is more valuable than treasure.** Mentoring and developing others creates reciprocity: *when you invest in people, they invest back in the team, multiplying results for everyone.*

I've always been motivated by incentive pay, a mindset I developed as a child. Risk and reward were part of my DNA. Over the years, I was fortunate to work with many talented people who shared that drive. While their risk was never as heavy as mine, their rewards were tied directly to their contributions, and together, we all prospered.

Sharing the fruits of success is one of the surest ways to keep people aligned toward a common goal.

A paycheck compensates time; shared rewards build ownership.

That principle is powerfully embodied in Jack Stack's *The Great Game of Business.* When he and his partners took over a failing division of International Harvester in Springfield, Missouri, they knew that survival required more than a turnaround plan. It required every employee to understand the financial game they were playing. Jack opened the books, taught his workforce the fundamentals of business, and empowered them to take ownership of the outcome.

Most contemporaries thought he was crazy. Yet, decades later, Springfield Remanufacturing Corporation grew from a single struggling factory into a diversified mini-conglomerate and an incubator for new ventures. His commitment to mentoring not only turned one company around but also influenced thousands more through The Great Game of Business, Inc. consulting and coaching activities.

I've followed Jack's teachings for years, and my own companies now practice his principles. The brilliance lies in its simplicity: **lead with transparency, teach with clarity, and reward shared success.** When people understand how they make a difference, they are more likely to rise to the occasion.

Giving Back to the Community

As an immigrant, I quickly came to appreciate the generosity of the American people. I have traveled the world, and nowhere have I found people more welcoming. This generosity is rooted in history: pioneers leaving home, cut off from family support, forced to form bonds with strangers to survive. Picture wagons circled against attack, neighbors standing shoulder to shoulder, whether or not they'd met the week before. That spirit remains in the American DNA.

Americans also carry a unique sense of **personal responsibility for others.** It's not about government redistribution; it's about choosing to lend a hand because it's the right thing to do. For immigrants, this generosity is a lifeline. You receive kindness, guidance, and opportunities from people who don't have to give them, and the natural response is to pay it back and forward.

Giving is not reserved for the wealthy. It might be a donation, a ride, a connection, or a piece of advice. Small acts of generosity ripple outward. As the saying goes: *To whom much is given, much is expected.*

My mission, and I hope yours, is to keep that spirit alive through mentoring, sharing knowledge, and being generous with time, talent, and treasure. Paying it forward is not just charity. It is the most reliable investment in the future, bringing us a deep sense of fulfillment and purpose.

I have derived great personal satisfaction from my work in educational guidance and governance at Drury University in Springfield. Established in 1873, this private institution was one of the first liberal arts colleges in Missouri.

My engagement started with an invitation to join the Breech Business School Advisory board as an international business representative. Per, a Swedish friend and former Drury swim team member and graduate, had been a member for years.

My advisory position lasted 12 years, during which time I gained significant insight into American higher education and had the chance to contribute my ideas.

I have been serving on the board of trustees for seven years. Drury graciously embraced me as a family member and allowed an immigrant to serve, helping current and future students have an even better, more relevant educational experience. Of course, our daughter is a Drury alum!

CHAPTER 14

NEDAP Consulting and Technology

While you certainly learn from your mistakes, there is nothing quite like success. My personal and business relationship with our client partner, NEDAP, sits at the very top of my list. I share this story not as a victory lap, but in the hope that it helps you recognize many of the key perspectives discussed in this book and, by example, encourages you in your own pursuit of success.

I am deeply grateful for the input from the two key individuals at NEDAP who helped launch and grow our collaboration.

In 2001, as the internet was becoming increasingly mainstream, I was actively seeking clients in Europe. One day, I came across an article in *Parking Today* magazine written by Evelien, the marketing manager of NEDAP's Identification Systems. The Dutch company was exploring the use of long-range RFID technology in the parking industry. Intrigued, I reached out and asked if they would meet with me at their factory in Holland. She agreed.

Within weeks, I was on a plane to Denmark, staying with my parents and borrowing their car to make the drive to NEDAP's headquarters in Groenlo. I was at the tail end of my severance package and taking a significant personal risk to pursue what was, at that point, little more than a promising possibility. But it was a risk worth taking.

At NEDAP, I toured their state-of-the-art facility, met their leadership, and asked countless questions. The company was in the midst of transforming itself from an OEM electronics supplier into a series of specialized vertical units, including long-range RFID.

There, in a spotless facility with laser-cut metals and climate-controlled labs, I saw the future. It stood in stark contrast to the scorching, noisy factory floors I had known. NEDAP's technology, particularly their in-vehicle transponder capable of authenticating drivers at high speeds, felt like a preview of what post-9/11 security infrastructure would demand.

After several conversations and trade show appearances, our discussions evolved quickly and laid the foundation for mutual trust. Within two months, we established a partnership to introduce NEDAP's long-range identification technology in the United States. Tuxen & Associates would serve as NEDAP's U.S. business development partner.

With NEDAP's brilliant engineering and management, combined with my team's business development efforts, we built a market from the ground up. Together, we became the leading provider of high-performance, long-range vehicle and driver identification technology in the Americas.

A key factor in bringing this venture to life was Jeroen Somsen's empathy and active engagement as managing director of NEDAP's Identification Systems. Jeroen championed our shared vision, advocated for it within his organization, and helped secure full management support throughout the entire due diligence process.

Jeroen writes the following summary of the early days of our collaboration:

Partnership in Motion

By Jeroen Somsen, Managing Director, NEDAP AVI (2001–2010)

When I think back on how NEDAP found its footing in the United States, one truth stands out: it wouldn't have happened without Gorm. What began as a few exploratory conversations turned into a partnership that reshaped our company's future and, frankly, my own perspective on leadership and risk.

From the very beginning, there was something intangible between us that I can only describe as chemistry. He brought an entrepreneurial fire and an instinct for execution that perfectly complemented my role inside NEDAP. I had the platform and the influence within headquarters; he had the conviction and the courage to take the leap. Together, we built the bridge that carried NEDAP across the Atlantic.

At first, Gorm's involvement was meant to be limited, with Tuxen & Associates serving as a consultant to help us assess market opportunities. But it became apparent within weeks that this wasn't a project to be advised from a distance. It demanded belief, commitment, and someone willing to take ownership. Gorm did precisely that. He didn't approach the opportunity as an outsider or vendor; he became a business partner, fully invested in the outcome.

At the time, NEDAP AVI was still in the early stages of scaling across Europe. Within the company, we were debating how best to accelerate: expand our product line, expand our geography, or both. Then Gorm appeared, and suddenly, those questions found their answer. What started as an exploration of a single market grew into a full-scale strategy for the Americas.

Our first major collaboration, partnering with the largest RFID card and door reader manufacturer in the United States, was the breakthrough moment. It gave us instant credibility, but what truly powered the expansion wasn't the technology. It was trust. It was the rare type of partnership built on equal parts friendship, belief, and shared purpose.

I often say that Gorm inspired me, but it's more accurate to say that we inspired each other. His drive and optimism were contagious. He saw potential where others saw limits. And in turn, I realized that my own belief in what NEDAP could become needed to expand. He helped me see that our most significant constraint wasn't the market, but our mindset.

Even now, years later, it's hard to pinpoint what exactly made our collaboration work so well. Perhaps it was the blend of personal respect, complementary strengths, and a shared vision that made us both better. Out of that mix came clarity, a plan, and, eventually, the execution that brought NEDAP's long-range identification technology to life across the Americas.

Looking back, I can say with certainty that the real catalyst wasn't a product or a market opportunity. It was a partnership that was rooted in trust, driven by purpose, and strengthened by friendship. That's what made the impossible possible.

Jeroen is now in his 37th year at NEDAP and is presently the managing director of Lighting Controls. In this position, he has led yet another department to new heights within the company, building on many of the lessons we learned together.

Growing a Narrow Product Line

We started with a very narrow product line in Long Range Vehicle Identification, consisting of just five items. On the surface, it didn't look like much. But I recognized something important: the NEDAP technology wasn't just another piece of equipment. It was an enabling technology, and if positioned correctly, it could open an entirely new market in perimeter access control.

That's precisely what happened. By focusing on how the technology fits into bigger systems, we created ten times the value of the hardware itself. For every piece of NEDAP equipment we sold, we developed opportunities for all the other components needed to build a fully automated access control system. Our partners, whether they sold or manufactured those pieces, suddenly had new markets to serve.

Here's the truth: without NEDAP equipment and the strategy we put behind it, those markets wouldn't have existed. The opportunity would have slipped by unnoticed.

Today, NEDAP's long-range access control is the leading product line in security, parking, and transportation across the Americas. The biggest distributors, OEMs, and integrators carry it. And it all started with five products and a clear strategy.

The lesson is simple: you don't need a massive catalog to build a big business. Sometimes, the narrowest product line, if you understand its potential and position it correctly, can open the widest markets.

It was a powerful reminder that **showing up in person creates bonds no technology can replicate.** Trust is built by handshakes, shared meals, and honest conversations, not by polished slides or virtual demos.

Even during the COVID-19 pandemic, when travel was impossible, I held onto that principle of staying connected. We transitioned to virtual training for installers and product managers, and what began as a temporary measure quickly evolved into a new division, *Connect Studios*.

The idea was simple: if we couldn't meet in person, we'd bring the backyard to them. We mailed out cornhole boards, recreating the casual feel of a BBQ, the kind of place where you'd laugh over a game and share a beer on the lawn. In a season defined by isolation, it gave our clients a sense of presence, of being seen, and it kept our relationships alive.

But even then, I knew: **technology can enhance trust, but only presence creates it.**

NEDAP Strategic Vision

At the time of my first engagement with NEDAP, the company was undergoing a fundamental transition from a long-standing OEM manufacturer and supplier of electrical and electronic components to a solutions-driven software, hardware, and services company.

Ruben Wegman had been hired as the head of a newly formed group of business units within the company, all slated to serve as initial points for what would become a complete transition of the company. Each business was headed by its own management group, which defined and built technology and relevance propositions for its industry and market. The overarching idea was to develop and integrate AEOS, a unified software platform for security management.

He brought his computer science credentials, extensive prior experience, and a plethora of new innovative ideas to the company. Appropriately so, the group was named the Ideas Group. NEDAP's Identification Systems Group, then known as "AVI," was part of Ruben's portfolio.

The "AVI" Group was a little different from the rest of the business units, as it was exclusively focused on developing markets for NEDAP's unique long-range reader and tag hardware technology as an accessory for any back-end system in the security, parking, and transportation industries.

I was incredibly impressed by Ruben's deep, innovative knowledge of technology and his vision for how it would change the company's future, and I was eager to learn all I could.

Mutual respect developed quickly as we sought out opportunities to be sparring partners. His innovative mindset matched mine: he was the absolute subject matter expert on technology, and I was the commercial challenger.

Another friendship formed, leading to much mutual learning and many challenging endeavors.

Today, Ruben has successfully led the company's transition and served as the CEO of NEDAP N.V. for the last 15 years. Here are some of his takeaways from our mutual journey.

NEDAP Consulting and Technology

By Ruben Wegman, CEO NEDAP N.V.

Gorm has been instrumental in building our current position in the U.S. market. Because of his European roots, he was able to explain to us, in a way no one else could, the key differences between doing business in Europe and in the United States. That clarity allowed him to quickly identify the essential elements of our go-to-market strategy that were holding us back in North America. With his excellent communication skills, he conveyed those insights exceptionally effectively.

One vivid example stands out. In Europe, suppliers often impose numerous conditions before a customer can return a product. So when we were negotiating one of our first supplier agreements with a key distributor, we struggled to accept a clause allowing them to return stock at any time, no questions asked. To us, it felt like a negotiation tactic. But Gorm was able to explain and persuade us that this was not a tactic at all, but a fundamental part of the U.S. "customer-is-always-right" mentality. It took some convincing at our headquarters in Groenlo, Netherlands, to accept this condition, but signing that supplier agreement ultimately proved essential to our success in the United States.

Many consultants support European companies entering the North American market by producing impressive plans. Where Gorm truly distinguishes himself is in his ability not only to design a strategy but to execute it. By taking the lead in establishing relationships with key market players and persuading American distributors to add NEDAP products to their portfolios, he demonstrated, beyond a doubt, the strength of our new go-to-market approach.

I have always admired Gorm's entrepreneurial spirit. But spirit without action means very little. What has consistently stood out to me is his stamina and perseverance. These qualities are essential for making the most of trade fairs and industry events. I have seen firsthand how Gorm, from the first prospect who enters the booth to the very last interested visitor, tirelessly engages with every single person, even while others are already tearing down their stands. His dedication, energy, and commitment to making every interaction count have always been defining parts of his character.

Another of his greatest strengths is his ability to distill complex products into simple, compelling messages. Like many organizations with many engineers, NEDAP tended to highlight as many technical selling points as possible. I will never forget how he explained what was needed. He said: "Listen. At this trade show, when a potential customer visits our booth, I will only get the time to give them three reasons to buy our product. So they better be good." This commercial insight has stayed with me ever since.

Over the years, I have not only enjoyed working with Gorm as a professional but also as a human being. His open personality and genuine interest in people made it easy to build a warm, personal relationship. Looking back, I am grateful for the trust, the conversations, and the sincere connection that developed naturally as we worked side by side.

CHAPTER 15

The Entrepreneurial Journey

Entrepreneurship is not just a career path; it's a way of thinking, living, and constantly adapting. Whether you're at the start of your venture, somewhere in the thick of it, or leading a mature organization toward new horizons, you're on a journey. And like any meaningful journey, it's not about getting from point A to point B in a straight line. It's about staying alert, flexible, and committed when the road disappears or shifts beneath your feet.

Entrepreneurs are the modern-day pioneers, embarking on a thrilling adventure. They pack up everything they own, leave behind the familiar, and set out into the unknown. Like those heading West, they carry only hope, determination, and a vision of what might be, braving uncertainty and challenges to build something entirely new. It's not just a career path; it's a thrilling adventure.

There's passion, yes.

Conviction, definitely.

But there's also unpredictability, constant learning, and an undercurrent of discomfort that you learn to welcome. You set off with a map in your head, only to realize halfway through that the terrain looks nothing like you expected. This adaptability is not just a skill; it's a necessity in the entrepreneurial journey, and it's what will keep you prepared and resilient when the unexpected happens.

So you pivot.

You re-pack.

You keep going.

In our businesses, we talk about "the journey" as more than just a metaphor; it's a framework for growth. It helps us align our vision with our purpose, anticipate challenges, and remain adaptable in the face of the unknown. With this mindset, we're not just reacting to change; we're actively preparing for it.

Let's journey onward into how this approach, driven by passion and pragmatism, shapes our strategies and sets us up for success.

Passion and Pragmatism

At the core of most entrepreneurial stories lies one word: passion. It's what fuels the late nights under dim desk lamps, the early mornings accompanied by freshly ground coffee, rising before the birds begin their search for the first worm of the day. Passion wakes you up with an idea and keeps you up when reality tests it.

But passion alone is not enough.

Left unchecked, it can mislead you, burn you out, or trap you in a cycle of chasing dreams without real progress. **That's where pragmatism**

comes in. The best entrepreneurs I've known learned to temper passion with practicality, to pair vision with strategy and emotion with numbers.

Pragmatism means tracking your numbers, not just because you have to, but because they speak a truth that passion sometimes drowns out. It means learning the language of finance, even if it doesn't come naturally. You don't need to be a CFO, but you do need to know whether your dream is financially viable, or if it's only surviving on adrenaline.

There's a reason only a small percentage of new businesses make it past the five-year mark. It's not because their ideas weren't good; it's often because the founder couldn't translate passion into a sustainable plan. It's easy to fall in love with your ideas; the real work is learning how to adapt them.

Entrepreneurship: A Team Sport

Maslow's pyramid, also known as the hierarchy of needs, outlines how humans must satisfy basic needs, such as safety and security, before they can focus on higher-level goals, including personal growth and achievement. In a startup, this means your team needs to feel stable and supported, with clear expectations, fair compensation, and a sense of security, before they can fully commit to taking risks or striving for innovation. If the foundation isn't solid, chasing higher-level goals won't matter. Ensure your team understands what they're signing up for and what they stand to gain, so they can take those risks with confidence and begin to execute the ideas.

From Idea to Execution

Every new venture starts with a great idea, something you believe in so deeply that you're willing to risk comfort, security, and maybe even your reputation for it.

But believing in an idea isn't the same as proving it. Early feedback often comes from supportive friends and family who want you to succeed. But supportive is not the same as strategic. And enthusiasm isn't validation.

You have to move quickly from belief to evidence.

Document your assumptions.

Challenge them.

Validate your assumptions through honest conversations with real customers. It's tempting to seek perfection before launching, but most businesses fail not because they launched too early, but because they launched without clarity. Your customers are your best guides, and their feedback is invaluable. It will reassure you and guide you in the right direction.

The good news is that testing your assumptions has never been easier. But with so much information available, discernment becomes key.

Know your sources.

Ask better questions.

Seek feedback from people who aren't invested in sparing your feelings.

And then, when you're confident your idea solves a real problem, simplify it. Make your message so clear that you can share it in the time it takes for an elevator to go from the first floor to the second. If people don't understand it quickly, they won't invest in it, financially or emotionally.

The market is your truth-teller. Be ready to adjust when it speaks.

Relevance Over Romance

Every entrepreneur starts out thinking their idea is unique, revolutionary, and necessary. But the market doesn't care how much time you've spent perfecting it. The market only asks: "Is this relevant to me?"

Relevance is earned through empathy, not assumptions. What problem are you solving? And who cares enough to pay for that solution?

It's not uncommon for startups to become so enamored with their innovation that they overlook the customer entirely. In my experience, most businesses end up becoming something different than what they first imagined. That's not failure. That's evolution!

If your initial idea has to be sacrificed for something better, let it go.

Flexibility isn't weakness. It's wisdom.

The faster you let go of old assumptions, the quicker you can grow something that works.

Bootstrap vs. Bailout

One of the most prominent modern myths in entrepreneurship is that success begins with funding. But asking others to risk their money before you've risked your own is not only unrealistic but also misaligned. Bootstrapping is more than a funding strategy; it's a mindset. It's about proving your concept through discipline, effort, and resourcefulness before seeking outside help.

Yes, capital is important. But capital should follow proof, not precede it.

Too many entrepreneurs waste precious time chasing investors when they should be focusing on customers. If you haven't yet created something worth paying for, you're not ready for investment; you're ready for refinement.

Freedom is one of the most compelling reasons people pursue entrepreneurship. But that freedom quickly disappears when control shifts to investors. Remember, whoever owns the risk often controls the outcome. Before you sell equity, know what you're giving up.

The earliest stage of a venture is survival.

So act like a Spartan: spend wisely, learn everything you can, and only bring on partners when they add true value, not just money.

If you can't afford professionals, consider becoming one yourself. Learn the basics of sales, finance, and operations on your own. That knowledge will make you a better leader and a better judge of talent when the time comes.

Build a Team, Not a Payroll

At some point, you'll have to scale. And that means building a team.

However, attracting good people isn't about titles or money; it's about **trust, transparency, and a shared vision.**

When we hire, we focus on three core principles: **attitude, aptitude, and altitude.**

We look for individuals who are excited to join the journey, capable of growing into their roles, and who understand the importance of the stakes.

Be honest with your team!

Don't oversell the vision without preparing them for the risks. If people are investing their livelihoods in your business, you owe them clarity, respect, and a fair share of the rewards.

Loyalty isn't given, it's earned.

Build it by thinking from the other side of the table.

Would you sign up for what you're asking of them? If not, rework the ask.

Mentor the Mission

As your team grows, so should your commitment to their development. Build a culture of mentorship, not micromanagement. Make the path forward visible and give people the tools to walk it.

Mentorship today also requires strong emotional intelligence, encompassing skills such as empathy, active listening, and conflict resolution. Many entering the workforce have grown up in a world dominated by screens, where face-to-face communication has taken a backseat. This makes leading by example more crucial than ever.

Show how to handle disagreements respectfully, such as actively listening to others' perspectives during a team conflict or using empathy to understand a colleague's challenges. By teaching these skills, you're not only helping them process issues but also equipping them to navigate and resolve conflicts with greater ease and grace.

People don't grow by accident. They grow when someone takes the time to invest in them.

Entrepreneurial Leadership

At some point in the entrepreneurial journey, building systems and strategies is no longer enough. You have to become someone worth following.

Genuine, authentic entrepreneurial leadership isn't about titles. It's about trust. It's about showing up with clarity when things get chaotic and helping others navigate uncertainty, not with bravado, but with presence.

In a fast-moving environment, the demands are constant and often contradictory. You're expected to make wise decisions in real-time, delivering both short-term results and long-term vision, often in the same sentence. People don't just want answers; they want confidence. And that confidence starts with how you communicate.

Your words matter. Your tone matters. Your timing matters. And when you speak, it needs to feel like it comes from a place of thought, not impulse. That's a hard-earned skill. Early on, I responded too quickly out of instinct, or pressure, or pride, and almost always regretted it.

Over time, I learned the value of taking a pause.

Of listening first.

Of filtering my response through a steady inner voice that took years to develop.

That inner voice saved me more than once.

There's a popular saying in leadership circles: "Trust your gut." I used to believe that. I don't anymore. Gut reactions are often just fast emotions in disguise. True discernment takes reflection.

One of my earliest leadership lessons came from a business school professor. On the first day of class, he walked in, said nothing, and lit a match. He held it until the flame got close enough to burn his fingers, then blew it out. Only then did he speak: "This is how long you have to make a lasting impression when you meet someone."

It stayed with me for over fifty years.

Because first impressions do matter. But keeping someone's trust takes more than a spark. It takes discipline, especially in how you carry yourself.

Listen before talking.

Ask before assuming.

Know when your silence speaks louder than your words ever could.

People are always watching, not in a paranoid sense, but in a human one. They're trying to decide, "Can I follow this person? Do they mean what they say? Would they do what they're asking me to do?"

You can't fake your way through those questions. You have to lead from the front. And you have to do it authentically. It can't be performative or forced. It just needs to be real, present, and grounded.

Leadership isn't about being perfect; it's about being intentional. It's about consistently showing people who you are and giving them a reason to believe that following you is worth it.

And when it's time to speak, speak from their point of view, not just your own.

Taking responsibility when things go wrong is one of the most critical parts of leadership. If you only learn at the point of failure and don't carry those lessons upward, the organization misses its chance to grow.

In my experience, it's always better when leaders own every failure, not just their own but those of the whole team. At the end of the day, it comes back to you anyway. You chose the people, you set the culture, and you decided whether risk-taking was encouraged.

That means when someone fails, they need to know you're standing behind them, not pointing a finger. When people feel safe to fail, they move faster, try harder, and grow stronger.

I've always believed that if you don't fail, you're probably not pushing hard enough.

When you show your team that you hold yourself accountable, they stop wasting time blaming circumstances or each other. They start asking, "What can I do better next time?" That's when failure turns into real progress.

On a personal level, owning your mistakes puts you in the solution rather than the problem. You can't control what you refuse to own, but when you take it on, you can shape the outcome.

Customer Service Is a Culture

We've entered an age where genuine customer service feels rare. In many ways, COVID-19 accelerated a retreat from high-touch service and a move toward automation and policy handbooks. But as companies stepped away from their customers, entrepreneurs were handed an opportunity: to stand out by showing up.

Customer service is not about being flashy. It's about being present. People still value being heard. They still want their needs understood and met. When you make service a cornerstone of your business culture, you gain something no marketing budget can buy: loyalty.

Retention always beats acquisition. A satisfied customer tells one person. A dissatisfied one tells nine. Make sure you're building an experience worth repeating.

The Journey Is the Destination

If entrepreneurship is a journey, then it rewards those who are prepared but not rigid.

Passionate, but not blind.

Visionary, but grounded.

The destination may change, but what matters most is the commitment to show up, stay flexible, and keep learning. **Success is rarely a straight line. It's a winding road that demands humility, resilience, and the courage to keep going when the map no longer makes sense.**

Let the journey teach you.

Let the market shape you.

Let your relevance keep you in the game.

Because, in the end, the journey isn't a path to the destination; the journey is the destination itself.

Conflict Resolution

And every real journey, no matter how exciting or purposeful, brings its share of conflict.

In business and in life, *conflict is inevitable.* You can design the most straightforward strategy, build the strongest alliances, and master time management. Yet sooner or later, you'll arrive at a crossroads where interests collide, emotions rise, and the stakes feel uncomfortably high.

The key is not to fear conflict, but to recognize it as part of the journey itself. Each disagreement offers a chance to deepen trust, clarify expectations, and strengthen relationships when handled with integrity and openness.

The First Reaction

When conflict surfaces, our instincts kick in fast. Fear, anxiety, anger, and defensiveness rush to the surface before logic can catch up. Depending on your personality and conditioning, you might react by counterattacking, searching for someone to blame, withdrawing, or flooding the moment with hurried words.

But the most effective leaders pause before responding. They understand that the first decision they make is not about *what* to say, but *how* to engage.

Choosing Your Path

At the first sign of conflict, you have three broad options: escalate it, walk away, or resolve it. The entrepreneurial mindset leans toward resolution, not because it's easy, but because it preserves relationships, reputation, and momentum.

To do this well, you must resist the reflex to defend. Instead, stop and analyze. Ask questions to uncover the true scope of the issue, the seriousness of the matter, and any contributing factors. **The aim is not to "win" the argument, but rather to understand it.**

By showing openness to dialogue, you can often surprise the other party, who may expect resistance or dismissal. This alone can shift the tone of the conversation and create space for progress.

Building Toward Resolution

Once the situation is clear, work toward a first point of agreement, however small it may be. This could be an acknowledgment of the facts, a shared goal for resolution, or simply agreeing on the next step in the process. From there, clarify responsibilities and outline specific actions to address the problem.

If blame is aimed at you or your organization, don't rush to accept fault before the facts are known. Take responsibility when appropriate, but only after the cause is fully understood. Prematurely claiming fault can create liability; avoiding accountability when it is warranted can erode trust.

Conflict as a Credibility Test

How you handle conflict often leaves a lasting impression that outlasts the conflict itself. If you lead the resolution process with clarity, respect, and fairness, you can walk away with not only a solution but also enhanced credibility with everyone involved.

And remember, conflict resolution is not a spectator sport. Avoid hiding behind email or text for difficult conversations. Pick up the phone. Better yet, meet in person. Tone, body language, and presence can dissolve tension that written words alone may inflame.

People are far less likely to be combative when you look them in the eye. By taking the risk of personal engagement, you position yourself not just as a problem-solver but as a leader worth following.

Tying It Back to the Journey

Conflict resolution, like time management, is about stewardship of relationships, trust, and shared goals. It's also closely tied to strategic alliances: the stronger your partnerships, the easier it becomes to navigate disagreements without losing the relationship.

Ultimately, every conflict you resolve with integrity strengthens your ability to lead. It turns potential roadblocks into milestones. And it ensures that when you and your partners face the next challenge, you do so on steadier ground—together!

Time Management

If you ask a room full of people what the most valuable commodity in the world is, you'll hear diamonds, gold, oil, maybe even data. But the honest answer? **Time.**

Time is the one resource we all have in equal measure each day, and the one we can never replenish. You can't buy more of it, bargain for it, or win it back once it's gone. What you *can* control is how you spend it.

Seeing Time for What It Is

Most of us prefer not to dwell on the fact that our total allotment of time, whether measured in years or minutes, remains unknown. But once you accept that, you can shift your focus from quantity to quality. The real question becomes, *Am I spending my time in ways that matter?*

In business, especially in the entrepreneurial journey, this isn't just a philosophical question; it's a survival skill. How you manage your time determines whether your vision gains momentum or grinds to a halt.

The Balance Between Speed and Patience

There's such a thing as moving too fast: burning out, missing details, and making avoidable mistakes. There's also the trap of moving too slowly, waiting for "perfect conditions" that never arrive. The sweet spot lies between those two rails, moving deliberately, knowing when to push forward and when to let ideas mature.

This means aligning your calendar with your priorities. It means planning, setting clear goals, and measuring progress. And it means cataloging what you've learned so each effort builds on the last rather than starting from scratch.

Respecting Time: Yours and Theirs

Growing up in Northern Europe, I learned that punctuality isn't just about being on time; it's about respect. Respect for the commitments of others. Respect for the shared journey. **In leadership, how you manage not only your time but also the time of those around you will shape your credibility.**

One of my biggest frustrations is the "aimless meeting," a gathering without a clear purpose, agenda, or outcome. Meetings can and should spark creativity, but without structure, they often devolve into pleasant conversations with no forward motion. Every meeting should end with clear notes, action items, and accountability, or you'll find yourself revisiting the same topics while real priorities go unattended.

Time as a Leadership Tool

High achievers, by nature, want to fill every moment with progress. But effective time management doesn't mean cutting out joy; it means ensuring the way you spend your hours aligns with your goals and values. Sometimes that means building in space for rest and reflection, so you can bring your best energy to the work that matters most.

In the entrepreneurial journey, time management isn't just about personal productivity; it's about stewardship. Every minute you use from your team's day is one minute they no longer have to achieve their goals. Treat that time as if it were gold, and guard it accordingly.

Because in the end, whether you measure success in revenue, relationships, or reputation, it all runs on the same currency: **time**. Spend it well, and you not only move your venture forward, but you also enrich the journey for everyone traveling with you.

Time management is about making space for what matters most. Once you master the discipline of guarding your own time and respecting others', you can turn that focus outward.

The next natural question becomes: Who should I be spending my time with?

That's where strategic alliances come in. Choosing the right people, companies, and organizations to travel alongside can determine not just the speed of your journey, but also its destination.

Strategic Alliances

In business, just like in life, you rarely get anywhere worth going entirely on your own. Entrepreneurship is an expedition, and every expedition needs companions. Strategic alliances are your fellow travelers, the ones who help you navigate unfamiliar territory, share the load, and sometimes even lead you to opportunities you wouldn't have found alone.

Think of the business landscape as an ecosystem. Every organism, including companies, customers, suppliers, and distributors, plays a role. The health of that ecosystem depends on the connections between them. **Strategic alliances are not just transactions; they're living relationships**. When they're strong, everyone in the network benefits.

Knowing Where You Stand

Before you can invite others on your journey, you must know where you are on the map.

- What role do you play in the bigger picture?
- Who benefits from aligning with you?
- And what do you bring to the table that makes a partnership more than just a handshake?

In my experience, entrepreneurs who thrive in alliances start with clarity and purpose. They know their value. They understand their gaps. And they can see where their journey intersects with someone else's mission.

Most of us won't start our venture with endless resources. Scarcity is often the reality. That's where alliances can change everything.

Choosing Your Path

Every go-to-market strategy is like plotting a route on a map.

- Will your product move through distributors, value-added resellers, or brick-and-mortar retailers?
- Or will you plant your flag online, building a digital presence powered by influencers and content creators?

Each path has its own unique terrain, investment requirements, and success checkpoints.

If your product or service is complex, your partners may serve as interpreters, helping translate its value into a narrative customers can understand. But that story must be tested. Field research is crucial here, just as it is in international markets. Assumptions, no matter how confident you feel about them, must be challenged against real-world feedback.

Partners Who See the Big Picture

The best alliances aren't just about immediate sales. They're about exchanging intelligence, opening doors, and sharing the market insights that can only be gained from people who've walked the road before you. They're not only helping you with tactical wins, but they're also shaping the strategic direction that keeps you relevant when the market shifts.

This is why alliance partners should be chosen as deliberately as a co-founder. They will influence your brand, your growth rate, and your ability to pivot when the unexpected happens.

Building for Mutual Benefit

Approach alliances with the mindset, "What can we build together?" not, "What can I get from this?" The strongest partnerships are those in which each party gains something tangible and both sides are invested in each other's success.

Early in your entrepreneurial journey, make identifying and nurturing these relationships a core priority. Like a seasoned traveler who chooses their guides carefully, surround yourself with people and organizations who know the territory you want to explore and are just as committed to reaching the destination.

When done right, strategic alliances don't just move you forward; they elevate everyone involved. They transform your journey from a solo trek into a shared adventure, where success is measured not just in miles covered, but in the strength of the company you keep.

CHAPTER 16

The International Business Journey

Going global isn't just about crossing borders; it's about crossing mindsets. And just like any meaningful journey, it doesn't begin with a polished roadmap. It starts with curiosity, discomfort, and a willingness to question everything you thought you knew.

Over the past five decades, I've had the opportunity to work in international business worldwide. **And I can tell you: no two countries, cultures, or conversations are ever the same.**

However, the biggest lessons weren't learned in boardrooms or on balance sheets; they came from the moments when I felt most out of place and had to learn how to listen better, adapt more quickly, and lead differently.

Let's unpack what it genuinely means to take your business global and how to do it without losing your footing.

Be Local to Think Global

When companies start looking abroad, the first instinct is to chase numbers. You analyze market size, demographics, and growth potential, all of which are good things. But spreadsheets don't tell you how people think. They don't tell you what they value, what makes them hesitate, or what makes them buy.

You can't export your mindset and expect it to work everywhere. What works well at home may not be effective overseas. To go global, you must first go local. That means studying culture before metrics, context before content.

Success in international business isn't about blending in, but about building bridges. It's about finding relevance, not dominance. And it always starts with a deep sense of humility, a recognition that you are a guest in someone else's world.

From Tourist to Teammate

Stepping off a plane into a new country doesn't make you global. It just makes you a traveler.

Your first real task is to observe, not to impress; not to sell, but to absorb. Whether it's your first or fiftieth time abroad, the rule remains the same: check your assumptions at the gate. Every culture has its rhythm, and your job is to find the beat without stepping on toes.

You're not there to be a tourist; you're there to build something real. *But you can't lead a market you don't understand.* That's why preparation is key, and presence matters. **The best way to avoid missteps is to show up with an open mind and a willingness to learn, not just about the business environment, but about the people themselves.**

And bring your team along for the ride. Not everyone will feel comfortable stepping into the unknown. That's normal. But discomfort is an influential teacher. Invite your people into the process. Let them catalogue the differences. Compare notes. Normalize the learning curve. When no one's expected to know it all, everyone becomes more willing to grow.

Start with the Right Questions

When entering a new market, the first questions aren't about sales targets or distribution plans. The first questions to consider are these:

- Who are we, really?
- How are we being perceived?
- What does this market need that we can uniquely deliver?

These aren't surface-level branding questions. They go deeper into your identity, your story, and your value. Because what worked in your home country won't always translate.

That quirky slogan?

That selling point you swore was universal?

It might fall flat or, worse, be misinterpreted entirely.

Imagine feeding a bunch of colorful crayons into a pasta maker. The result? Strips of pasta that no longer look or function like crayons. That's what happens when your message travels without context. What goes in is not what comes out.

So slow down.

Rethink the narrative.

How can we present ourselves in this new market in a way that makes sense to them, not just to us?

And then, start small. Enter through one focused segment.

Learn.

Listen.

Adjust.

Your first steps will teach you more than any market report ever could.

Communicate Like a Guest, Not a Local

Language is more than words. It's culture. It's cadence. It's nuance. And in international business, miscommunication is less a matter of "if" than "when."

Even English, spoken globally, splinters into different tones and meanings depending on whether you're in the U.S., U.K., South Africa, or Singapore. And when English isn't the native language, the risk of misinterpretation increases exponentially.

This is why clear, intentional communication matters. Whether verbal or written, it's not just about what you say, but also about how it lands. One misunderstood sentence can derail a deal. One poorly timed joke can close a door you didn't even know was open. So approach every conversation like a guest at someone else's dinner table: respectful, attentive, and ready to listen more than you speak. Clear and respectful communication is crucial in international business, as it fosters trust and understanding.

Act Like an Ambassador

Going global means becoming an ambassador, not just for your company, but for your values, your brand, and your way of doing business. That role requires more than knowledge. It requires a curious mind that is always eager to learn about new cultures and business practices.

Be the one who asks questions, not just about logistics, but about people, customs, and context. Locals will often be more than willing to teach you if they see that you're genuinely curious, not just transactional.

You don't have to pretend to be local. But you do have to care. The best ambassadors aren't fluent in every dialect; they're fluent in human connection.

And here's something I've learned: people will often remember how you made them feel long after they've forgotten what you pitched.

Fail Close to Home Before You Go Far Away

There's a temptation, especially among startups and early-stage companies, to expand globally quickly. The idea of conquering new markets is exciting. But it's also risky.

Before you take your business halfway across the world, make sure you know who you are at home. Your team, your systems, and your product: test them where the cost of failure is lower, and the learning curve is familiar.

Once you've built that foundation, international expansion becomes a logical next step, not a hopeful leap.

For more established companies, international markets often represent untapped growth. But even then, the same principles apply: stay humble, stay curious, and stay flexible.

What the World Can Teach You About Business

International business is a journey, not a destination.

It will test your assumptions, your communication, and your patience. But if you approach it with the mindset of a learner and the discipline of a builder, it will reward you with insights, partnerships, and growth you never imagined.

Remember, success abroad doesn't come from replicating what worked at home. It comes from rethinking what's possible in a new context.

So pack your bags, bring your humility, and keep your eyes and ears wide open.

Because the world isn't just waiting to buy from you.

It's waiting to teach you something.

CHAPTER 17

Sales: The Journey from Value to Victory

In entrepreneurship, there's one measure that cuts through the noise of projections, pitch decks, and strategy sessions: **sales**.

Not just any sales, but sales that create both top-line growth and bottom-line strength. Revenue without margin is a race to exhaustion. Margin without volume is a business running on fumes. The sweet spot, where volume and value meet, is where an entrepreneurial venture truly thrives.

Throughout my career, I've learned that the days of selling solely on product features and benefits are behind us. In today's market, commodity selling, where price is your primary competitive lever, is a dangerous game. Competing on price alone forces margins into a narrow and often unsustainable range, especially for startups that need every ounce of profit to reinvest in growth and expansion.

If you find yourself in "shark-infested waters" surrounded by competitors, survival depends less on cutting prices and more on defining a value proposition that competitors can't easily copy.

The Shift to Value-Added Selling

Value-added selling isn't just a sales technique; it's a mindset. It starts with aligning your product or service to something bigger than itself, positioning it as part of a solution that matters deeply to your customer. This requires building a narrative that answers the customer's most important question: *Why should I care?*

Marketing and sales are often lumped together, but they serve distinct purposes. Marketing is the **strategic foundation**, the knowledge base, research, and positioning work that defines your channels, pricing, and communication strategy. Sales is the **tactical execution**, the art of bringing those strategies to life, engaging directly with customers, and closing deals. Marketing shapes perception; sales turn that perception into a signed agreement and a deposit in your account.

One without the other is incomplete. Brilliant marketing without sales execution is just noise. Skilled sales efforts without a clear marketing strategy are wasted energy.

Sales as a Learning Engine

Selling is not a one-way pitch; it's a two-way discovery process. Each sales conversation is a fact-finding mission, a chance to test your relevance against honest market feedback. The insights gained here should inform your marketing strategy directly, ensuring that your message evolves in line with the market.

This is where many entrepreneurs miss an opportunity. They treat sales only as the act of closing business, rather than as an ongoing intelligence operation that keeps them tuned to customer needs, competitive shifts, and emerging opportunities.

The Human Element in a Digital Age

Technology, especially artificial intelligence, has transformed how we find leads, analyze markets, and even craft outreach. These are powerful tools, but they're not substitutes for the human element. AI's answers are drawn from the public domain, not from the proprietary, hard-earned knowledge that comes from direct engagement with your customers.

The best entrepreneurs "trust but verify." Use AI to accelerate your process, but validate its outputs against the reality you've gathered from honest conversations in your market. AI can point you toward opportunities; only human engagement can confirm they're worth pursuing.

Sales as the Lifeline of the Journey

If you can't sell your product, you need to diagnose the problem honestly:

- Is it a relevance issue? Does the market truly need what you're offering?
- Is it a marketing issue? Are you failing to reach and persuade the right audience?
- Or is it a sales execution issue? Are you not effectively connecting, demonstrating value, and closing the deal?

Each diagnosis leads to different actions, but they all come back to the same truth: sales validate your entire entrepreneurial process. Every closed deal is proof that your product matters, your message resonates, and your execution works.

Tying It Back to the Journey

Sales connect to every other part of the entrepreneurial journey. Without time management, you can't focus on the activities that generate revenue. Without strategic alliances, you limit your reach and opportunities. Without effective conflict resolution, you risk losing key customers over solvable issues.

And without sales, you have a hobby, not a business!

Sales is not the end of the journey. It's the fuel that keeps the journey going, the confirmation that the path you've chosen is worth walking. Approach it as a craft, a conversation, and a constant learning process, and you'll not only close deals, but you'll build a venture that lasts.

But closing deals is only the beginning. Sales prove that your idea has a place in the market, yet what happens next is even harder. **Growth will test everything sales validated: your resilience, your systems, and your ability to manage people, capital, and time.** If sales are the lifeline, growth is the crucible where businesses either stabilize or collapse.

That is where our journey turns next.

Challenge and Response Mapping

Different people look at their past in different ways. They develop perspectives depending on the vantage point they choose and how they catalog or view their life's challenges and responses.

As I was writing this book, I was challenged to illustrate my journey as a means for others to be inspired, to take stock of their own challenges in life and in business, and to learn how to respond to them.

In the process, I developed a small tool for me to better illustrate my timeline, challenges, and responses. You will find that included in the following illustration.

It dawned on me as I was doing this that this methodology could be used by anyone looking toward the future while being informed by their past. I hope you find it useful. If I lost you in the preceding narrative, this might help set you back on course as far as trying to understand my journey.

While this roadmap paints a very positive picture of how I dealt with my challenges, it was not accomplished without periods of doubt, confusion, and grief, sometimes seeming too heavy to overcome. But by God's grace, I managed to keep looking toward the future and eventually turned negatives into positives.

Challenge Response Map

Year	Stage in Life	Challenge	Response	Growth
1957	Born - Copenhagen, Denmark		Entrepreneurial and loving upbringing	Learned how to recognize and embrace the support of family
1964	Middle-school	Bullied in school	Withdrawal/distrust	Became a dreamer
1971	Trade prep school	Failed acceptance to College Prep School	Improved grades and entered College Prep the next year	Learned the relevance of formal education
1972	College prep school	Catching up academically	Doubled down on my studying	Building knowledge to grow independence
1974	Accident	Picking up the pieces	Take charge of the family	Converged into adulthood
1975	US exchange student	Adopt to a new culture	Immersed myself in the opportunity to become one with my new environment	Found clear alignment between my values and those of America
1976	Danish college	Culture challenges	Became a culture warrior for Compassionate Capitalism and the U.S.	Expanded my effectiveness in standing up for my beliefs
1979	Danish Hardwood, Apprentice	Declining health	Focused on job performance	Resiliency both physically and mentally
1980	Private grad school	Educational bridge to goal	Expanded on my knowledge of the U.S. and executed to plan	Performing to goal despite health challenges
1982	**Immigrated** Domino Furniture	Build from nothing	Traveled thousands of miles by car, canvassing the market	Learned how to build mutually beneficial business relationships.
1984	Married	Making America a viable home	Grew understanding of the strength and commitment of a loving partner	Embraced the blessings, challenges and commitment required in married life
1986	Eurostyle Furniture	Business start up and failure	Realized impending failure and managed to it	Learned humility in a very real way and the need to manage by your financials
1989	Experimental Surgery	Failing Health	Received life altering surgery for my chronic bowel disease.	Stayed in control of failing business during surgery and recovery
1990	Pen Trading	Turn around	Stayed focused on what was ahead rather than what was behind me.	Trusting in the fact that something will come if you look hard enough
1991	Duncan Consultant	Learning while Teaching	Understood what I knew and did not know and developed plan to learn	Listen to learn
1994	V.P. DMS	Develop Integrated Software	Explore market needs	Learned a lot about solutions relevance and software development
1996	Director Duncan	Deploy Integrated Solutions	Established a new standard for on street parking management.	Learned to operate successfully in highly politicized environment
2001	Established Tuxen & Associates	Independence	Set out to gain independence though partnerships rather than employment	Recruiting and growing success for foundational client
2007	Established Tuxen Integrated Systems	Security IT Infrastructure	Built on previous experience to design enterprise systems to open standards	Designing to scale
2011	Established IPsens	Parking/Transportation IT Infrastructure	Developed enterprise parking occupancy hardware and software solution	Improved understanding of risk/reward in developing niche applications
2023	Established Tuxen Group	Multi Company Management	Developed management structure to facilitate growth in multiple companies	Learned how to enable new generation of leaders
2025	Author/Entrepreneur	New Horizons	Sharing experiences with others for them to use as inspiration in their own journey.	Learning how relevant I might be in this pursuit.

Immigrant Entrepreneurship In America

CHAPTER 18

Business Growth and Maturity

From side hustle to sustainable business, growth is the point where an entrepreneur's dream either takes root or falls apart. It's where the lessons of frugality, resilience, and courage are put to the ultimate test against the harsh reality of payroll, leases, and cash flow. It's also where you learn the most brutal truth of all: growth doesn't forgive mistakes; it magnifies them. But with resilience, these challenges can be overcome.

Growth: The Hungry Stage

Growth isn't just about more sales. It's about managing resources like cash, people, products, and time as if your life depends on it. Because in many ways, it does.

When my wife and I opened our Scandinavian furniture store in Nashville, we didn't think of it as an MBA case study. It was survival. At first, it was just the two of us. Then, little by little, family joined in: my sister, my cousin, my brother-in-law, and, eventually, a bookkeeper. That was the team.

But before we sold a single chair, we signed a lease for 10,000 square feet of retail space. We signed personal guarantees, paid the first and last month's rent, and made utility deposits. Then came the $100,000 in inventory shipped across the Atlantic. Our big idea was immediate fulfillment: everything in stock, no waiting. That meant buying in bulk, even if it meant betting everything we had.

Had it not been for our Danish partners, Ole and Arne, who also happened to be our suppliers, agreeing to a consignment arrangement, we wouldn't have lasted a month. They weren't just vendors; they were mentors and risk-takers who believed in us enough to put their own money on the line with ours. This is a lesson every entrepreneur should remember: growth isn't fueled by transactions. It's fueled by trust, the cornerstone of any successful business relationship.

A year in, we had already learned two painful truths:

1. **Our product mix wasn't enough.** Customers wanted upholstery to complement our bookcases and dressers. Without it, we weren't relevant.
2. **We were in the wrong location.** We had bet on a major road expansion that never came. Twelve months into a five-year lease, with over $100,000 invested in advertising and no traffic, it was clear. Location can bankrupt you before customers ever get a chance to.
3. And then came the third lesson: **Cash flow is king.**

It doesn't matter how good you are. If you run out of oxygen, the game is over.

We borrowed against inventory, signed personal guarantees we barely understood, and clawed our way into downtown Nashville, a better location with more promise. However, when the late-1980s financial crisis struck, we had no reserves left to weather the storm. We closed the business in an orderly fashion and started over.

The math is brutal, and every entrepreneur eventually learns it: once you're behind on cash flow, there's no working harder to catch up. The mountain only grows taller.

The Cost of Growth

Every business type carries its own weight:

- **Retail** demands inventory. Money is tied up until the sale is complete.
- **Restaurants and groceries** deal with perishables; unsold products are not just wasted, they're gone forever.
- **Manufacturing** requires machinery, raw materials, and long lead times. One forecasting mistake can cripple the entire system.
- **Services** account for payroll as the most significant expense. Miss that, and your people who never signed up for your risk pay the price.

The details change, but the principle stays the same: growth will drain more than it gives, until the business finds its footing. That's why bootstrapping, while painful, is often the best way to maintain control. If you bring in outside partners, make sure they are more than checkbooks. They need to be co-risk takers. And banks? They're not in the business of risk. Neither are venture capitalists.

Cash, people, relevance. Guard them with your life.

Maturity: Building to Last

Reaching maturity feels impossible when you're in the trenches of startup life, but it's the goal you keep in sight. A mature business doesn't just fight to survive; it learns to optimize, innovate, and expand without compromising its core values.

Here's what that looks like in practice:

1. Reinvest in Innovation

Mature businesses die when they stop taking smart risks. I saw this in furniture when Domino introduced knockdown furniture, which consisted of flat-pack boxes that customers assembled at home. It cut shipping costs and opened a whole new market. It was a glimpse of IKEA before IKEA became a household name in America.

Years later, in the parking meter industry, we pioneered software that integrated meters, enforcement, and maintenance into one system. In security, we introduced high-speed, long-range vehicle and driver ID, an advance that became crucial after the tragic events of 9/11.

With the world's largest outdoor retailer and resort operator, we broke single-source lock-in by designing and deploying open integration solutions standards, potentially saving millions in future equipment replacement costs while boosting both efficiency and security.

The lesson is the same across decades: Innovation doesn't mean reinventing everything. It means reengineering what exists to meet needs no one else has noticed yet.

2. Deepen Customer Relationships

Customer service isn't a department. It's the heartbeat of a mature company. Customers forget when everything goes right, but they never forget when someone cared enough to fix it when it went wrong.

Our model has always been engagement: before the sale, after the sale, in training, in support. Technology has helped us, but it has never replaced human connection.

Listening creates loyalty. Loyalty creates longevity. This is the power of customer relationships in business maturity, a testament to the value of every customer and their loyalty over time.

3. Explore New Markets
For decades, Tuxen & Associates helped European firms enter the Americas. Every new market required humility: translating manuals into Spanish, setting up local representatives in Mexico, and adjusting the strategy for South America.

You can't just export what worked at home.

Each market deserves respect, attention, and cultural understanding.

4. Optimize Core Operations
Lean processes aren't just for startups. A mature business must keep learning how to do more with less.

Efficiency is the engine of cash, and cash is the engine of growth.

5. Pursue Partnerships and Acquisitions
The fastest way to test your relevance is through collaboration. Partnerships let you experiment without committing to the wrong path. Mergers and acquisitions (M&A) can enhance capabilities or acquire new customers when organic growth slows, but only if they align with your purpose.

6. Refresh Your Brand
Markets evolve. So must you. But don't abandon what made you matter in the first place. Sometimes it's not about becoming something new;

it's about explaining your value in a way that resonates with today's audience.

7. Leverage Data and Digital Tools
From dashboards to predictive analytics, data helps you anticipate instead of react. *However, numbers alone don't drive growth; people who know how to interpret them do.*

8. Invest in People and Culture
Every innovation, every customer relationship, and every new market depends on one thing: people. Invest in them. Train them. Mentor them.

Culture is the glue that holds maturity together.

Building the Bridge Forward

Looking back, I see a thread running through every stage of my journey: growth is never guaranteed. It demands sacrifice. It humbles you with failure. And if you last long enough, it teaches you that maturity isn't about size or even profitability.

Maturity is about resilience; it's about building something that can withstand storms, pivot when needed, and still serve people with integrity.

Growth asks: *Can you survive?*
Maturity asks: *Can you endure?*

And the answer depends on how well you've managed the only three things that ever truly matter in business: **cash, people, and trust.**

From Basement Office to Lasting Legacy

I first learned about legacy from my father, not because he tried to craft one for himself, but because he lived in a way that left a mark on others.

He invested in people, shared his wisdom freely, and put service before self. By the time he was done, his legacy wasn't etched in bank accounts or buildings. It was written in the hearts of those he had lifted along the way. What greater legacy could anyone want?

That lesson profoundly shaped me, but my own growth also came through learning to accept mentorship from others. Over the years, I have gathered a long list of mentors, partners, and influencers whose guidance has helped me shape my perspective, avoid unnecessary mistakes, and accelerate my maturity. Learning from other people's challenges, defeats, and victories gave me a perspective that no textbook could offer.

Eventually, I found myself moving from student to mentor. And truth be told, that transition has been one of the most rewarding parts of my journey. When I founded Tuxen & Associates, I made it a priority to build a culture of mentorship into the company's very DNA. **One of my earliest criteria in hiring was simple: find people who were eager to learn, who listened well, and who valued growth as much as outcomes.**

That's how I met Curtis Dennis. He had just completed his MBA at Drury University and was interning at a local Target store. I interviewed him in the cafeteria, not wanting him to walk into the basement office of my house and realize he would be the only employee. I was on my way out of town, but I knew enough to recognize potential. I offered him the job, preparing him for small beginnings and uncertain days. To my relief, he said yes.

Curtis quickly absorbed everything I shared, bringing with him a gift for systematic process development and careful research. He became the bedrock of the company's administration and growth, eventually rising to the rank of associate partner after more than 20 years of loyal service.

Not long after hiring Curtis, he introduced me to his college roommate, a high-energy, extroverted individual who became our first salesperson. He thrived under the same mentoring culture, eventually moving on to lead economic development at the Springfield Chamber of Commerce and later becoming an entrepreneur in his own right. Watching him build a clothing store and microbrewery with his wife was a proud moment, proof that our investment in people pays dividends far beyond the company walls.

A few years later, a local restaurateur connected me with Nate Leech, who walked into my office with strong people skills, eagerness to learn, and ambition to grow. Nate not only succeeded as a salesperson but also personally recruited much of our team, developed training programs, and became our other associate partner.

Today, Curtis, Nate, and I continue to lead the company together, carrying forward a culture of mentoring that ensures continuity and growth. Over the years, many of our employees have moved on to bigger opportunities, each leaving behind a legacy of their own contributions. Not one of them left empty-handed; they took with them lessons, confidence, and the ability to make an impact wherever they went.

What began in a basement has become a living legacy of mentorship, growth, and shared success. Just as I once received guidance from those who came before me, I now see the most significant measure of my legacy not in what I've built, but in the people I've had the privilege of mentoring.

The greatest reward isn't what you achieve, it's who you help grow along the way.

Growth teaches you discipline, resourcefulness, and resilience. But in time, every entrepreneur discovers that even the best-managed business is only part of the story. What matters most isn't just surviving payroll or scaling operations; it's what endures after the numbers fade. Beyond profits and partnerships, the actual return on investment is the impact you leave on the people around you: employees who grow, families who flourish, and communities that benefit from your work.

That is the real test of maturity, and it points us toward the deepest reward of all: legacy.

CHAPTER 19

Emergency Management: Spin Control

Imagine yourself as a pilot. You are flying on a clear day, relaxed and confident, headed toward a few days at the beach with friends on board. The trip feels routine. You check the forecast; the sky looks harmless; and everything appears in order. But as you continue forward, the light begins to shift. Clouds form on the horizon. The air grows heavier. Then the engine gives a faint sputter you have never heard before—not dramatic, not alarming, but enough to make you focus.

Every pilot understands that the sky never guarantees stability. Conditions can change with little warning, and the difference between a manageable challenge and a life-altering emergency is determined long before the trouble appears. It is defined by how far ahead of the airplane you have chosen to fly.

Preparation is not optional. It is a discipline of anticipating, evaluating, and maintaining awareness before anything becomes critical. Business operates by the same rules. Entrepreneurs who spend their days reacting only when problems surface eventually develop tunnel vision. They become locked into the tasks they know best and overlook the subtle signals that something is shifting.

A technologist may believe innovation alone keeps customers returning. A sales-driven founder may become absorbed in interactions, campaigns, or service. Those strengths matter, but they cannot replace the one instrument panel that must always remain in full view: your financials. Numbers tell the truth about the aircraft you are flying. Ignore them, and the clouds you failed to notice will eventually take control.

I have experienced enough close calls to know why preparation matters. None of those moments destroyed me, but every one of them shaped me. People often ask how I managed to recover from the emergencies I faced. The answer is simple: I stayed ahead of them as best I could. Emergencies never arrive at a convenient moment. They require calmness, discipline, and a clear understanding of priorities.

And in aviation, those priorities are taught in a method every pilot remembers.

In aviation, the following methodology is taught for setting priorities in managing and developing emergencies.

1. Aviate
2. Navigate
3. Communicate

These three words have guided countless pilots through the worst conditions imaginable, and they apply just as directly to entrepreneurship.

Aviate

Your first responsibility is always to fly the airplane. When something unexpected happens, the instinct is to lock onto the problem and forget everything else. Pilots feel this urge as strongly as anyone, but if you stop flying, the situation will decide the outcome.

Business follows the same pattern. When challenges appear, your priority is to keep operations stable. Continue serving, delivering, and supporting customers. You can analyze the situation and shape a response, but you cannot abandon the fundamentals that keep the business airborne. You must keep flying the airplane.

Navigate

Once the aircraft is stable, the next question becomes clear. Where am I, and what are my options?

In business, this means assessing how much runway you have left, what resources remain, and what alternative paths you can take if your first plan fails. As the weather worsens, fuel becomes the most critical factor in any cockpit. Fuel is life. In business, fuel is cash. When financial clouds gather, the first place to look is your numbers. They tell you whether you have the room to adjust or whether you need an immediate course correction.

Navigation is about finding the safest path through uncertainty. Avoid the darkest part of the storm, conserve your resources, and locate the nearest safe place to land.

Communicate

Pilots are trained to declare an emergency early, not late. Air traffic control cannot help you if they do not know what you are facing. Silence is not a strategy; it is a risk.

Business requires the same transparency. Your team, partners, and advisors are your ground controllers. Sharing the truth builds trust and reassurance. Clear communication creates alignment. Alignment creates stability. When conditions are shifting, people do not expect perfection from you. They expect honesty and direction.

Sometimes, even with proper preparation, you still come in fast, land hard, and walk away shaken. The airplane may be damaged beyond repair. The runway may appear only at the last moment. But if you walk away, you survive. Gratitude becomes the first response.

A business crash rarely ends a founder's life unless the founder decides it will. You recover physically, mentally, and emotionally. Then you evaluate what happened, gather the lessons, and rebuild your strength. Eventually, you return to the runway better prepared for the next flight.

Failure is humbling. It exposes what you did not know and encourages reflection on what you might do differently next time. When examined honestly, failure becomes experience. It strengthens your judgment and sharpens your instincts. I know this from my own history. None of my failures destroyed me. All of them shaped me.

The purpose of this chapter is not to create fear of turbulence in flying, business, or life. It is to remind you of a truth every pilot learns sooner or later. Emergencies rarely appear without warning. There are signals for those willing to notice them, systems for those willing to prepare, and a path forward for those willing to stay calm and proactive.

The sky will not always be smooth. Your business will not always fly in clear weather. But with preparation, perspective, and the discipline to stay ahead of the airplane, you can navigate far more than you think. More often than not, you will walk away from the landing wiser, clearer, and better prepared for the next flight.

CHAPTER 20

Meaningful Rewards

What legacy really means. Success isn't just about income or status; it's about impact, contribution, and the life you build for the next generation.

Legacy is the ultimate measure of growth. I first learned this lesson from my father, not because he set out to craft a legacy for himself, but because of the way he lived his life. He put people first, invested in their growth, and freely offered his wisdom. By the time he was done, his legacy wasn't carved in buildings or bank accounts; it was written in the hearts and minds of everyone who had crossed his path.

What greater legacy could anyone want?

Defining True Rewards

It's easy to get lost in the chase for recognition, wealth, or status. Capitalism, when misunderstood, can appear to be a game where the rich win and everyone else loses. But when applied correctly, capitalism can be the engine of shared growth, providing the resources and opportunities to build a lasting legacy.

When fueled by vision and incentive, it creates opportunity for families, teams, and communities. It allows people to see how their contributions build not just profit, but value. This value can be passed forward, extended beyond the founder, and carried on as a living legacy.

The entrepreneurs who risk everything for a dream and invite others into that vision deserve credit. They take on risk not only for themselves, but for those who are willing to walk alongside them. And when those journeys succeed, the rewards are more than financial; they are communal, generational, and significant, binding us all in a shared narrative of success.

Legacy isn't what you leave behind; it's what you build into others that carries forward.

Value That Lasts

Legacy isn't measured by the amount of money you leave your children. It's measured by whether you leave them stronger, wiser, and better able to help themselves and others. A true legacy sets in motion a ripple effect, like rings in the water, spreading opportunity and resilience far beyond the initial circle of influence.

This is the kind of value worth pursuing: not temporary gain, but enduring impact. This is the type of impact that builds a future, sustains a community, and continues to grow long after the founder's time running the organization.

America's Living Legacy

This idea of legacy isn't limited to individuals. The United States itself embodies it. Like a person, the country has aged and evolved, sometimes violently, often controversially, but always with lessons to be learned.

The gift of freedom has given each generation the chance to stumble, to rise, and to pass on the wisdom of both defeats and victories. This is a living legacy that we all contribute to and benefit from.

If we interpret history honestly, it becomes a powerful mentor. It teaches us how to live more wisely, build stronger families and teams, and leave our successors better prepared. But to learn, we must resist the temptation to rewrite history in reverse.

Legacy is about listening, remembering, and carrying forward, not erasing.

Building Your Own Legacy

Ultimately, meaningful rewards are not about wealth or recognition, but about the contribution one makes. Your legacy is the sum of the lives you've touched, the values you've passed on, and the opportunities you've created for those who come after you.

May you go on to build a legacy that lives in the hearts of others. May you embrace the hard lessons of your journey, and may you have the satisfaction of looking back, not only at what you achieved, but at how much you poured into others.

Half a century ago, I peered out the window of a plane and saw icebergs drifting south of Greenland. They were massive, silent, and humbling reminders that most of life's weight lies beneath the surface. At the time, I didn't know what awaited me in the United States. All I had was a suitcase, a body weakened by illness, and a heart determined to build something new.

Looking back, I realize those icebergs were more than scenery. They were a metaphor. Like an immigrant's life, like an entrepreneur's journey, most of the strength lies in what you don't see. Beneath every visible achievement is a hidden mass of sacrifice, resilience, risk, and faith.

That's the immigrant mindset.

It's about starting again when the odds say you shouldn't. It's about embracing humility in the face of failure, cultivating gratitude in small wins, and the courage to build when nothing is guaranteed. And it's not reserved for those who cross oceans. **Anyone can choose to think like an immigrant: to see opportunity in adversity, to value what is real, and to build a legacy that outlives them.**

My story is just one version of that truth.

The real invitation is yours.

What will you build?
Who will you lift?
What legacy will you leave in the hearts of others?

Ultimately, success is not about the titles you earn or the wealth you accumulate; it is about the impact you make. It is about the lives you touch, the values you embody, and the courage to keep moving forward when the path isn't clear.

That is the legacy worth striving for.

And that, above all else, is the meaningful reward.

As I close this book, I want to end not only with the universal but also with the personal. The lessons of resilience, risk, and legacy are not just ideas I've written about; they are threads woven through my own family. No story of my journey would be complete without honoring the two people who walked beside me and gave my life its most profound meaning: my wife, Anette, and our beautiful daughter.

EPILOGUE

A Tribute

A case study in family business

When I think about resilience, partnership, and legacy, I picture my home. For over four decades, Anette has been my anchor, walking beside me through every risk, setback, and new beginning. Together, we've raised a daughter who embodies the courage and compassion that shaped our journey. This story wouldn't be complete without honoring Anette, my wife of 41 years. Through every challenge and triumph, she has been the steady force behind everything we've built together.

We met in Denmark in 1982, while I was finishing my master's degree. I knew almost instantly she was the one. And in what I still consider one of my most successful "strategic acquisitions," I did everything I could to ensure she would become mine.

From the very beginning, Anette proved that she wasn't just my life partner, she was my business partner. At only 22, newly married and fresh out of college, she became vice president of our first company, Eurostyle, and ran the sales floor at our Nashville furniture store. She had an instinct for style, an ear for what customers wanted, and the grit to keep pushing even when the odds weren't in our favor.

When Eurostyle closed, she carried us through the next chapter. She worked for an interior design firm that built Saturn dealerships nationwide, keeping our family afloat while I navigated corporate transitions. Later, when our daughter Emilia was born, Anette chose to stay home to raise her with the same focus and care she had poured into our businesses.

But the entrepreneur in her never stayed quiet for long.

One evening in 2000, sitting around the dinner table with friends, the talk turned, as it often does in entrepreneurial homes, to new ideas. By the time dessert was cleared, Anette and a partner had each written a $500 check to launch a gift shop called *Gift House*. She wanted the freedom to build something while still having Emilia by her side.

Like any new venture, it was on a road of discovery, finding the right products, the right market, the right rhythm. Eventually, she saw a bigger opportunity. In 2001, while I was in Europe visiting my ailing father, Anette called with news: she had found a new location in Branson, Missouri, right on Highway 78, the main strip lined with theaters and drawing millions of tourists a year. She had already met the landlords, started negotiations, and envisioned a pivot: moving from gifts to ladies' fashion.

By 2002, *Fashion House* was born.

She struck a smart consignment deal with suppliers, bootstrapped the business, and generated positive cash flow almost immediately. What began as a small store grew steadily into a premier upscale women's boutique, serving southwest Missouri and northwest Arkansas. Today,

Fashion House is a cornerstone in downtown Branson, employing a dedicated team and supporting the local economy.

And Anette hasn't just survived the hard seasons, she's reinvented them. When COVID-19 shut Branson down in 2021, she didn't hesitate. Within weeks, she launched live online sessions to reach customers from the comfort of their own homes. "Tempting Tuesdays," her weekly Facebook event, now reaches thousands of people every week and has become a defining feature of the brand.

What makes me proudest is not just the business she's built, but the way she built it with courage, creativity, and an unshakable commitment to people.

Our daughter, Emilia, has since joined the family journey, bringing her communications degree to Tuxen & Associates as head of marketing and communications and serving as controller for the Tuxen Group. Watching her step into leadership beside us has been one of the greatest rewards of all.

Our daughter has also brought us the immeasurable gift of our beloved son-in-law, Ethan, and our precious grandson, Oakland.

It's not often that a husband gets to say his wife is his partner, his co-founder, and his inspiration. But I can. Anette's strength, vision, and relentless drive have shaped not only my career but also our family's legacy. I am proud beyond words of her, of our daughter, and of the life we've built together.

The truth is, no legacy is built alone. Mine has been woven together by faith, partnerships, friends, and family, first with my parents, sister, and brother, then with Anette by my side, and now through our daughter, who carries forward the same courage and compassion. **If this book has**

shown anything, it is that resilience is not just an individual story but a shared one. And as you write your own story, may you find the same strength in those you love, and may your legacy echo in the lives you've touched.

This may be the end of the book, but it is not the end of my journey. I'll leave you with one parting thought:

Entrepreneurship has no finish line. Every sunrise is another blank page, and every challenge is another chance to build, to risk, and to grow. What you create today becomes another point of reference for tomorrow's journey, a journey that never truly ends. Remember, *perspective depends on your vantage point, so do not dwell on failure; it takes care of itself. Instead, find the vantage point from which you can see success.*

Acknowledgements

Writing this book has been very therapeutic for me and hopefully leaves you, the reader, with something of value. If nothing else, it certainly allowed me to work through the broom closet to dust off history, look at the bookmarks, and revisit all the lessons learned on my journey.

Everyone has a journey; you must catalog your lessons as you move along. Doing this can provide you with a library of key points and blessings that may be worth keeping for later reference.

Let me start by expressing my deep gratitude to my angel writer, Sarah Ruddle, an ordained minister and accomplished business professional in her own right, with a record of proudly serving in the U.S. Army Intelligence before earning a doctorate in business. She brought this book together beautifully. I am proud to count her among my friends.

My thanks to everyone who contributed to the book, reviewed the first drafts, and offered suggestions. And of course, everyone at Authors on Mission who helped manage the publishing of this book.

Special thanks go to Jack Stack, CEO of SRC Holdings and author of *The Great Game of Business*, for taking an immediate interest and offering to write the foreword, and to John Beuerlein, General Partner at Edward Jones for 50 years and former Drury University President and Emeritus Trustee, for his friendship and for providing further encouragement and a thorough review. The support of such accomplished individuals truly humbles me.

Sincere thanks to my parents, who raised my family and me, for always believing in my dreams. My team, my colleagues, clients, and friends who supported me on the journey to become a successful immigrant entrepreneur—I could not have done it without you.

Special thanks to my lifelong friends Ebbe Greve, Gene Scobey, and Dan Walsh. You were always there, come rain or shine.

Great gratitude and thanks to:

Ole Antonsen, who took a chance on sending me to America for Domino Furniture and taught me how to become a sales professional, and later became our partner in Eurostyle. You are a friend for life. And to Arne Prentow, in memoriam, Ole's and our partner for years, for his great operational talent.

Richard T. Farrell, in memoriam, for being the best boss anyone could want in a large corporation, while at Duncan. Jerry Scalpone, Sr. for enabling me to learn as much as I could about software development at Duncan Management Solutions and, subsequently, for his partnership in IPsens.

Jeroen Somsen for catching the ball early on in our partnership with NEDAP, and to Ruben Wegman for his staunch support for over two decades. Both business partners and friends, what more could anyone ask?

Curtis Dennis and Nate Leech, Associate Partners at Tuxen & Associates, for their journey with me, evolving from students to mentors and leaders in their own right.

Last but not least, thanks to Donald Hancock for partnering up on the physical integration and implementation of Tuxen Integrated's marquee security solution design project. We demonstrated great expertise, made a big difference, and became close friends in the process.

To learn more about our businesses and services you can visit us at www.tuxengroup.com

To contact and learn more about Gorm, please visit his page on LinkedIn.

www.ingramcontent.com/pod-product-compliance
Lightning Source LLC
LaVergne TN
LVHW010331070526
838199LV00065B/5724